MARTIAL VIRTUES

MARTIAL VIRTUES

Lessons in Wisdom, Courage, and Compassion from the World's Greatest Warriors

CHARLES HACKNEY, PHD

TUTTLE PUBLISHING
Tokyo • Rutland, Vermont • Singapore

Published by Tuttle Publishing, an imprint of Periplus Editions (HK) Ltd., with editorial offices at 364 Innovation Drive, North Clarendon, Vermont 05759 U.S.A.

Library of Congress Cataloging-in-Publication Data

Hackney, Charles H.
  Martial virtues : lessons in wisdom, courage, and compassion from the world's greatest warriors / by Charles H. Hackney. -- 1st ed.
      p. cm.
  Includes bibliographical references.
  ISBN 978-0-8048-4023-1 (hardcover)
1. Martial arts. 2. Spiritual life. 3. Martial arts--History. I. Title.
  GV1101.H33 2010
  796.8--dc22
                                    2008055785

Distributed by

North America, Latin America & Europe
Tuttle Publishing
364 Innovation Drive
North Clarendon, VT 05759-9436 U.S.A.
Tel: 1 (802) 773-8930
Fax: 1 (802) 773-6993
info@tuttlepublishing.com
www.tuttlepublishing.com

Asia Pacific
Berkeley Books Pte. Ltd.
61 Tai Seng Avenue #02-12
Singapore 534167
Tel: (65) 6280-1330
Fax: (65) 6280-6290
inquiries@periplus.com.sg
www.periplus.com

First edition
14 13 12 11 10   10 9 8 7 6 5 4 3 2 1

Printed in Singapore

Contents

1

Martial Arts and the Character of the Warrior

To set the cause above renown,
To love the game beyond the prize,
To honour, while you strike him down,
The foe that comes with fearless eyes;
To count the life of battle good,
And dear the land that gave you birth,
And dearer yet the brotherhood
That binds the brave of all the earth.

Sir Henry Newbolt

Martial arts without martial virtue
are useless for the ways of warfare.

Nakae Toju

Those who aspire to train in the Way of Karate must not
focus only on the technical aspects; they must also seek to
cultivate the spiritual aspects of the Way, since true
karate-do trains both mind and body.

Gichin Funakoshi

As long as there have been warriors, people have held to the idea that certain qualities of character separate a warrior of excellence from one who is merely skilled at violence. In the 4th century BCE, the philosopher Plato discussed this concept in his *The Republic* (Book II, Chapter 3). Society's guardians, Plato argues, would turn on the community, and on each other, if their aggressive natures are not shaped and guided by other qualities, such as gentleness and a love of learning.

In the 5th century AD, the legacy of Bodhidharma established a connection in China between martial training and spiritual development, in which Buddhist compassion and enlightenment were fused to the warrior arts. In 12th-century France, Bernard of Clairveaux lauded the virtues of the Knights Templar, calling them an ideal mixture of Christian holiness and martial fierceness, and thus superior to ordinary self-serving knights. George Silver, the 16th-century English defense master, writes in his *Paradoxes of Defense* about the value of martial training as a method of personal development: "[Training in weapons] gives a perfect judgment, it expels melancholy, choleric and evil conceits, it keeps a man in breath, perfect health, and long life... it makes him bold, hardy and valiant."

In the early 17th century, the young samurai Tashiro Tsuramoto recorded the teachings of the elder samurai Yamamoto Tsunetomo in a book known as *Hagakure*. In that volume, it is said that a samurai is incapable of fulfilling his role as a retainer if he does not possess "enough compassion within his heart to burst his chest."

In the 19th century, Jigoro Kano's adaptation of Jujutsu into Judo was designed to be a vehicle for character development in young people, through the teaching of principles such as self-control, discipline, respect, and of course the *ju* principle of yielding flexibility. World War II veteran and philosophy professor Sidney Axinn, in his 1989 book *A Moral Military*, focuses on each individual soldier as a moral agent, describing military honor in terms of courage, honesty, justice, fidelity, and self-sacrifice. The warrior's character is an idea that crosses centuries and crosses cultures, Newbolt's "brotherhood that binds the brave of all the earth."

And to this day, countless martial arts instructors promote their training, promising character development along with physical fitness and self-defense. One has only to look at the telephone book advertisements, the flyers, the websites, and the storefront designs of the majority of dojos to see claims that, in addition to learning the physical components of the art, psychological traits such as discipline and self-esteem are intended to be derived from the training. Parents are urged to send their children for lessons, educators are proposing martial arts programs as a means of rehabilitating violent adolescents, and some psychotherapists incorporate martial training into their work as an adjunct to more conventional forms of therapy.

Clearly, the connection between positive character traits and the martial arts is an idea with ancient roots and modern influence. It is also a bidirectional connection, in that martial training is described as a method of enhancing one's character, and positive character traits are described as necessary for martial advancement.

Gichin Funakoshi, founder of Shotokan Karate, incorporated principles of character development into the basic structure of his system. He considered them vital to advancement in Karate, and to this day many Shotokan students recite the "dojo kun," a five-line summary of Funakoshi's ideals, at the end of every class.

Bujinkan Budo Taijutsu is a traditional Japanese system with a combined ninja and samurai heritage. While many Japanese styles draw heavily from the *bushido* ideal of the samurai, moral thought within the Bujinkan is more heavily influenced by its Ninjutsu roots, and the accompanying philosophical approach known as *ninpo*. Bujinkan writings and teaching consistently intertwine ninpo principles with the physical techniques, as it believed that the same mindset that makes one a better person also makes one a better fighter.

In her book *The Sovereignty of Good*, Irish novelist and philosopher Iris Murdoch puts forward the idea that the fundamental enemy of moral living is the "fat relentless ego" of humanity's inherent selfishness. Every one of us lives with this enemy. It is that part of each of us that screams out "me first" and demands to be satisfied no matter who gets hurt along the way (and that includes hurting oneself in the long term to gain satisfaction in the short term). From the smallest indulgences to the greatest cruelties, the fat relentless ego wins every time someone cuts off another driver in traffic, every time a young bully uses the pain and humiliation of his victim for his own entertainment, every time a husband cheats on his wife. Murdoch argues that the goal of moral philosophy is to develop techniques to aid in the defeat of the ego. In large ways and small, our egos demand that we put ourselves above others, and the better we get at saying "no" to the ego, the more morally advanced we become, and the more fully human we become.

Is there a place for the martial arts in the defeat of this enemy? The purpose of this book is to explore the possibility, employing the combined resources of the psychological research literature on the development of positive character traits and virtue ethics, drawing primarily from the work of moral philosopher Alasdair MacIntyre.

MacIntyre distinguishes between what he calls the "qualities of effectiveness" and the "qualities of excellence." The qualities of effectiveness are what enable a person to achieve rewards such as status, riches, prestige, and power. However, attaining these rewards is not what makes one a *good* practitioner of an activity. A scientist who falsifies data in order to obtain a large research grant and employment at a prestigious university, a police officer who plants evidence in order to secure a conviction, an Olympic athlete who "wins" a gold medal by cheating, a politician who rises to high office through deception; these people may be successful, if they are skillful enough to avoid being caught. But by no stretch of the imagination would we consider these people to be examples of a *good* scientist, police officer, athlete, or politician.

The qualities of excellence, on the other hand, are what enable one to be a *good*, not just successful, practitioner of an activity. These qualities are referred to as *virtues*, and in the examples given above, the missing element is the virtue of honesty.

Similar statements could be made about the martial arts. Qualities of body and mind exist which enable a person to win fights. Strength, speed, and technical skill are among these qualities. These qualities are desirable, and necessary for the excellent fighter as well as the effective fighter. Alone, however, they are insufficient to qualify one as a *good* martial artist. To be a *good* martial artist, the qualities that make one effective must be augmented and guided by qualities of character such as compassion, courage, and self-control.

In some cases, the qualities of effectiveness and the qualities of excellence overlap. Self-control, for example, is necessary for a dishonest politician who wishes to convincingly lie to the public. In the martial arts, as well, some qualities of effectiveness may be identical to some qualities of excellence. One obvious example of this would be the virtue of audacity, which is the courage to boldly execute techniques in the face of an opponent's attack.

In other cases, the qualities of effectiveness and the qualities of excellence stand in opposition to each other. Hypocrisy in politics is seen as a quality of effectiveness, exemplified in Machiavelli's insistence in *The Prince* that a great leader must always appear to be moral, but must never truly be moral.[1] A hypocritical politician is able to deliver contradictory messages to different audiences, change positions with the shifting of public opinion polls, and develop self-justifying arguments to excuse almost any action. Skillfully executed, this pattern can be employed to

---

1. "So a prince need not have all the aforementioned good qualities, but it is most essential that he appear to have them. Indeed, I should go so far as to say that having them and always practising them is harmful, while seeming to have them is useful... It must be understood that a prince and particularly a new prince cannot practise all the virtues for which men are accounted good, for the necessity of preserving the state often compels him to take actions which are opposed to loyalty, charity, humanity, and religion."

the advancement of the politician's career. However, hypocrisy is not a quality of excellence in politics. The politician who speaks truthfully and directly, and who makes policy decisions from a set of steadfast principles, may be at a disadvantage during election campaigns, but is exactly the kind of person that voters want in positions of leadership.

An example of this opposition in the life of the warrior is the quality of compassion. As will be seen in our survey of various approaches to the warrior virtues, compassion in one form or another is almost universally prescribed for a warrior of excellence. However, compassion may sometimes result in defeat, and military victory may be gained through acts of cruelty.

The use of biological warfare may be an example of victory through cruelty, such as the siege of Caffa in the year 1346, in which the Mongols loaded plague-infected corpses into trebuchets and hurled them into the city. A similar example is Pontiac's Rebellion in 1763, in which British soldiers gave smallpox-infected blankets to a delegation of Delaware Indians during the siege of Fort Pitt, resulting in an epidemic among the tribes of the Ohio valley.

An example of compassion interfering with victory is the story of Marcus Luttrell. In June of 2005, Luttrell's SEAL team was in Afghanistan, hunting Taliban leader Ahmad Shah. The team encountered three Afghani civilians, whose knowledge of their actions endangered the mission. The team was divided over whether to kill the civilians, removing the potential danger but violating the rules of warfare, or to let them go and risk a Taliban attack. Luttrell cast the deciding vote, choosing to let them go. As they had feared, soon after releasing the civilians, Taliban forces attacked and killed the SEALs, with only Luttrell surviving. In 2006, Marcus Luttrell was awarded the Navy Cross for his actions, and his decisions serve as reminders that an act of compassion will not always lead to a military victory. A warrior who demonstrates cruelty rather than compassion may be victorious, but we would not look to this person as an example of a *good* warrior.

This book is my inquiry into the question of what it means to be a good warrior: someone who possesses the qualities of excellence, not just of effectiveness, in the martial arts. In doing so, I will be primarily drawing from the psychological literature on the development of character strengths, and from the philosophical literature of virtue ethics. I will begin by giving in Chapter Two an overview of virtue theories, both philosophical and psychological. That chapter will be followed by an examination of historical and scholarly literature on the qualities of the ideal warrior, from which our list of warrior virtues will be developed. Five virtues will compose our list: courage, justice, temperance, wisdom, and benevolence. Each virtue will be examined in turn, with an emphasis on how each virtue is supported and enriched by the other virtues, how we can work to cultivate that virtue within ourselves, and how we can assist in the cultivation of that virtue in others.

The word "virtue" comes from the Latin word for "power," and like all forms of strength, virtues grow stronger through exercise. Exercising the virtues enters us into an "upward spiral," in which we grow stronger every time we defeat the fat relentless ego, and every increase in power results in greater ability to defeat the ego in our next confrontation. Because virtue theories rely so often on images of combat and strength, I suspect that most warriors will see a natural fit between their training and the language of virtue ethics. It is my hope that this book will be of use to students of the martial arts who wish to explore possibilities for the cultivation of their character within the context of training, to instructors of the martial arts who wish to enhance the character-formative component of their instruction, to psychologists who wish to follow others' examples and incorporate martial training into programs intended to foster mental health, and to those with an interest in character development who wish to consider the role that the martial arts may play in the shaping of personalities.

2

Virtue Ethics, Positive Psychology, and the Martial Arts

Virtue is a state of war, and to live in it we have always to combat with ourselves.

Jean-Jacques Rousseau

The sword and the good should go hand in hand.

Masaaki Hatsumi

The Fall and Rise of Virtue Ethics

In order to examine the character of a warrior from the perspective of virtue ethics, we must begin by tracing the development of that field. Any time someone talks about an admirable trait such as honesty or bravery, or holds up another person as a model of "good character," that person is employing the language of virtue. Ideas concerning what kinds of character traits make someone a "good person" are as old as moral thought itself. These ideas appear across cultures, in all major religions, in classic works of philosophy, and in everyday conversation.

Scholarly attention to the virtue perspective, however, experienced centuries of decline and neglect. The period of Western history known as the Enlightenment (roughly the seventeenth through nineteenth centuries) saw a rejection of this line of thought by many of that movement's prominent thinkers. As we will see below, virtue theories center around a vision of the ideal life, and this did not fit well with Enlightenment philosophy. Enlightenment philosophers wanted to rely entirely on objective rational analyses that flow unquestionably from self-evident first principles, and a vision of an ideal life is neither objective nor self-evident.

The Enlightenment saw a shift of focus away from the question of how to be a good person, and toward a question of method. Instead of asking "what kind of person should I be?" they asked "how do I make good choices?" This decision-centered approach to ethics has become so common that it may surprise some readers to learn that ethical philosophy can be applied to areas of life other than solving moral problems. In the Enlightenment's problem-centered approach, ethics are not required at all until you come to a situation in which more than one possible moral option exists. You shift into an ethical mode of thought, decide which option is the right one, and then shift out of the ethical mode of thought and back to business as usual. Alasdair MacIntyre, in describing 19th-century moral philosophy, puts it this way: "morality was a distinct and relatively autonomous area... *The* moral was sharply and clearly distinguished from *the* aesthetic, *the* religious, *the* economic, *the* legal, and *the* scientific."

To illustrate this, consider the overall approach taken when modern ethics are applied to matters of professional behavior and social policy. Should a medical experiment be performed if there is a risk to the participants? Should the death penalty apply to convicted murderers with an IQ below 65? Should teenage girls be required to inform their parents before having an abortion? The common factor in all such issues is that they are dilemmas, and it is assumed that the purpose of ethical theory is to provide guidelines for resolving these dilemmas. By the consistent appli-

cation of well-grounded ethical principles, Enlightenment thinkers argued, solutions to such problems can be found.

The two major theoretical camps in Enlightenment-influenced
ethics are rule-focused ("deontological") and outcome-focused
("consequentialist") in nature. The first of these ethical theories
tells us that problems will be solved through the consistent application of the correct rules. This approach is primarily associated with the philosophy of Immanuel Kant. If the proper rules of
behavior can be specified (for example, "Psychotherapists should
never sleep with their clients."), then ethical dilemmas can be successfully resolved. When this kind of ethical thought is put into
practice, the result is usually a list of dos and don'ts governing
how to handle various situations.

Many martial arts organizations follow this procedure. The To-
ronto-based Academy of European Medieval Martial Arts (AEM-
MA), for example, operates according to a set of nine "Rules of
the Salle D'Armes," and being familiar with these rules is a part
of advancement in rank within that organization. It is presumed
that adhering to these rules will ensure a good training environment for all involved. The rule that forbids recruits (low-level students) from engaging in sparring bouts before their fifth month
of training protects participants from out-of-control attacks. The
rule forbidding foul language in the academy guards against hurt
feelings. Such lists of rules are attempts to apply universal principles (such as the importance of safety and the demonstration of
respect) to members' conduct, providing everyone with guidance
in making decisions in the situations to which the rules apply.

One of the major arguments against this approach is that specific situations often do not precisely fit the rules. In regards to
AEMMA's rule forbidding profanity, for example, there are ways
to express disrespect that do not include obscene words, making
it quite easy to be within the "letter" of the law while violating the
"spirit" of the law.

How much flexibility should be built into the ethical system? If
a student at an AEMMA-affiliated training group accidentally lets

a curse slip when painfully struck with a training sword, should that count the same as obscenity as an expression of disrespect? When should an exception be made to a rule? Should AEMMA's rule about not permitting recruits to spar be applied if the recruit has had many years of experience in a different martial art? How many exceptions can be made before the rule is no longer a rule? If new rules are made to cover new situations, is there ever an end to the making of new rules? And, does it make any sense at all to make a rule that one should not be too rigid in the application of the rules?

Consequence-focused ethics, on the other hand, takes a different approach to making moral decisions. This approach, associated with such thinkers as Jeremy Bentham and John Stuart Mill, focuses on the outcome of a situation, and the idea that the right answer to any ethical dilemma is whichever option produces "the greatest good for the greatest number" of people.

For example, a doctor is treating a set of conjoined twins, and the twins are at risk. If she separates the twins, one will die. If she leaves them together, both will die. Looking at these possible outcomes, the correct answer is to sacrifice one twin so that the other will live. The right decision is the one with the best results.

Applying this approach to issues involving the martial arts might be seen in the morality of self-defense, especially if the topic is the use of lethal techniques in defense of yourself or of another person. Some martial artists, drawing from a rule-focused perspective, would argue for establishing a set of guidelines about what kinds of combative reactions are permissible in different self-defense situations. Others, though, might echo the sentiments of Bujinkan Shihan Bud Malmstrom, who once said that "the only rule in a real fight is waking up on the right side of the grass." Instead of asking the question of whether or not harming (and possibly killing) another person fits the rules, the question becomes a matter of outcomes. If you do not fight, what might happen? If you do fight, what might happen? If your opponent is just a posturing twit, then the consequences might be minimal. But what if the situation is more serious, with more severe results for fighting or not fighting? In extreme self-defense circumstances, the argument could be made that the greatest good for the greatest number could include the death of an attacker, not only in terms of saving your own life, but also in terms of saving the lives of the attacker's future victims.

Seventeenth-century samurai Yagyu Munenori put it this way: "It may happen that a multitude of people suffer because of the evil of one person. In such a case, by killing one man a multitude of people are given life. Would this not be a true example of the saying that 'the sword that kills is the sword that gives life'?" This statement is a clear example of how an outcome-centered ethical approach would look at the morality of killing.

In the same way that there have been many objections to rule-based ethics, there have also been many objections to consequence-based ethics. One of these objections is that it is impossible for anyone to really know all the possible outcomes of an event. We might guess, but there are always unknowns at work. It doesn't seem very rational to make decisions by comparing one set of unknown outcomes against another set of unknown outcomes. This is especially problematic when we are talking about killing another human being. Who can predict how someone's life would have been led if they had been allowed to live? We may argue that they *might* go on to kill numerous people, but we can't know that for sure.

While numerous objections (beyond those mentioned here) have been raised about these ethical approaches, at a fundamental level many have objected to the over-emphasis on rationality in both of these forms of ethics. Critics argue that a life of moral excellence is not achieved through legalism, or the robotic calculation of pros and cons. Logic is good, but is logic everything? What about concepts such as being wise, or having a kind heart? These things are terribly hard to measure, and usually do not fit neatly into calculations, but most people consider them to be of great importance to moral living. With growing dissatisfaction over these two dominant ethical approaches, several scholars within the past few decades have increasingly given attention to a third possibility: virtue ethics.

Alasdair MacIntyre: Virtue Ethicist

While many scholars have made great contributions to the revival of virtue ethics, the name most often cited as central to the movement is moral philosopher Alasdair MacIntyre, and his 1984 book *After Virtue*. As such, *After Virtue* will serve as the primary philosophical resource for this exploration of warrior ethics.

In *After Virtue*, MacIntyre traces current problems in ethics and public moral debate to the failure of Enlightenment-influenced theories to make good on their promise to rationally justify a universal morality. Unable to agree on first principles, we have no way to secure common agreement over specific moral issues (abortion, euthanasia, war, etc.). Being "right" on such issues in our modern context becomes a question of effectiveness at securing and maintaining power by persuading the majority of voters to agree with you, by persuading persons in positions of authority to agree with you, or by acquiring enough wealth to unleash teams of lawyers on whoever stands in your way.

Reviving Aristotle

Having traced the failure of Enlightenment ethics, MacIntyre argues in favor of a return to Aristotelian thinking, a movement referred to as "neo-Aristotelian" philosophy. Overall, the neo-Aristotelian approach may be considered a description of the ideal human life, and of the ways and means of moving from our current state toward this ideal state. The Aristotelian approach can be understood by learning three Greek words: *telos, eudaimonia,* and *aretê.*[2]

---

2. Because of the importance of these terms, Aristotelian philosophy is sometimes referred to as "teleological," "eudaimonic," or "aretaic" in nature.

Telos. *Telos* is typically translated as "end," "goal," or "purpose," and it refers to the built-in functioning of some object. A description of the *telos* is the answer to questions such as "What is this for?", or "What does it do?" The *telos* of a clock is to tell time. The *telos* of a wolf is to hunt as a member of a pack.

A description of the *telos* also provides a standard for describing something as good or bad. A good object fulfills its purpose well. A good clock keeps time accurately. A good wolf cooperates with the pack. If an object does not fulfill its purpose, we are safe in calling it "bad." If your clock never keeps time accurately, it is a bad clock. A bad wolf does not coordinate hunting tactics with the rest of the pack, and therefore will be a less effective predator (the reason that a "lone wolf" is dangerous is that it is most likely starving and so is more likely to do something desperate).

So if clocks and wolves can be evaluated in terms of their function, can we do the same for humans? The "Big Question" for one who adopts an Aristotelian perspective is: What is the human *telos*? Aristotle argued that, since it is rational thought that makes humanity unique among animals, the human *telos* is found in the exercise of our rational capabilities. Those who operate within a religious worldview find their description of the *telos* within theological statements concerning the purpose of humanity. Virtue ethicists who operate from non-theological perspectives claim that the human *telos* involves functioning well as social animals, and in the exercising of abilities that evolved as survival-related adaptations.

Eudaimonia. For Aristotelian thinkers, the best kind of life is one that is spent getting better and better at fulfilling the *telos*. *Eudaimonia* is often translated as "happiness," and refers to "a complete human life lived at its best." This definition of happiness centers around completeness and optimal functioning, so it is not the same as the hedonist's definition of happiness (the state of experiencing more pleasure than pain). Growing into a better and more complete person requires hard work and sacrifice, a concept with which martial artists should be intimately familiar.

Aretê. Aretê is the Greek word that we translate as "virtue." Alasdair MacIntyre defines virtues as "those qualities the possession of which will enable an individual to achieve *eudaimonia* and the lack of which will frustrate his movement toward that *telos.*"

Virtues are character traits that enable someone to be a highly functioning person. Virtue ethicist André Comte-Sponville puts it even more strongly: because the virtues are qualities of excellence for humans, the more virtuous one becomes, the more human one becomes.

Plato is credited with presenting one of the classic lists of the virtues. In *The Republic*, Plato describes what we call the four Cardinal Virtues (wisdom, justice, courage, and temperance), which he conceptually connects to the components of a properly ordered society. Plato's list of Cardinal Virtues has had a tremendous impact on moral philosophy through the centuries including, as we will see, on medieval conceptions of the chivalric virtues. Following Plato's lead, the great medieval philosopher/theologian Thomas Aquinas developed a list of seven virtues in his *Summa Theologica*; Plato's Cardinal Virtues, plus faith, hope, and love.[3]

In the next chapter, we will be discussing the possibility of producing our own list of virtues through an analysis of current and historical ideas of what it means to be a warrior. This analysis will follow the same approach as a recent study done by research psychologists, who engaged in a cross-cultural study of major philosophical and religious traditions such as Christianity, Confucianism, Islam, ancient Greek philosophy, and Hinduism. The results of their research indicate that six virtues (courage, justice, humanity, temperance, wisdom, and transcendence) tend to be endorsed in one form or another around the world and throughout history. In the next chapter, I will be examining multiple martial traditions for virtue ideals that warriors worldwide tend to have in common.

---

3. Many other examples are possible, including lists of virtues produced by Prudentius, Cicero, David Hume, and Benjamin Franklin.

Without exception, scholars who have examined the virtues have stressed the notion that the virtues tend to "intertwine with and reinforce each other." This intertwining nature of the virtues is a theme that will run through this book, emphasizing not only how each virtue contributes to one's development as a warrior, but also how each virtue interacts with the other virtues in a relationship of mutual enhancement.

Most scholars (but not all) have attempted to construct some sort of hierarchy, claiming that some virtues are "higher" than others, and many of these scholars identify a highest "master virtue" that shapes and informs the others. Examples include love, practical wisdom, the Buddhist virtue of emptiness, and the Christian virtue of *kenosis* (self-emptying).

The Aristotelian approach to philosophy has rapidly expanded lately, finding an appreciative audience in a wide range of academic and applied fields such as education, organizational studies, theology, and military ethics. The question for us is: can we follow in this tradition and develop an Aristotelian approach to the martial arts?

Where do the Martial Arts Fit Within MacIntyre's Approach?

In *After Virtue*, MacIntyre describes the virtues as being social in nature. A description of the human *telos* is developed through the interactive discussions of a community's members (Aristotle would not have been able to build his philosophy without other Greek philosophers to debate with), and the virtues are cultivated through social action.

MacIntyre uses the term "practice" when discussing the kinds of community-based activities that help people to cultivate the virtues. The pursuit of excellence in a practice provides benefits at the level of the individual's life and the level of the universal good of humanity. It is by engaging in practices, developing one's virtues as a member of those practices, that we develop the virtues that shape our lives, making us better human beings.

It is through activity as a member of practices that I develop the virtues that constitute my character. As a psychological researcher, I learn honesty by always reporting my findings truthfully, and I learn humility by not pretending that my small contributions to the advancement of the field mean that I know all there is to know about human nature. As a professor, I show justice by giving my students the grades that their work deserves, and I learn wisdom by perceiving what I must do to assist my students in the learning process. Someone who lives a different life, and engages in different practices (for example, a psychologist who works in a mental health clinic rather than at a university), will not develop these virtues in precisely the same way that I do. Though they may possess the same virtues, their characters will be unique (a wise professor and a wise clinician will have different kinds of wisdom).

If these are qualities of character that I learn as a practitioner of psychological research and of teaching, then what about as a practitioner of the martial arts? In what way does the practice of the martial arts contribute to my development as a person, assisting me in my ongoing battle with the "fat relentless ego"? Within this process, from the level of a practice to the level of an individual life to the level of universal human nature, how can the martial arts facilitate my development toward the overall human *telos*? In other words: ***Can the martial arts help make me a good person?***

The bulk of this book is dedicated to addressing this question. In the next chapter, I will attempt to develop a list of the warrior virtues, with the perspective that cultivating these virtues as a practitioner of the martial arts will assist in the cultivation of the same virtues within the context of one's life, which in turn assists in the movement of the martial artist toward the universal human *telos*.

The Virtues in Positive Psychology

Virtue ethics is one of the two major scholarly influences on this book. The other major influence is the "positive psychology" movement. This movement in psychology officially began with Dr. Martin Seligman's 1998 tenure as President of the American Psychological Association. Positive psychology is "the study of the conditions and processes that contribute to the flourishing or optimal functioning of people, groups, and institutions." Think of it as a way to examine with a psychological lens the same kinds of topics that virtue ethicists examine with a philosophical lens.

Positive psychologists argue that most of the time and resources used by mainstream psychology has focused on the many ways that humans can go wrong, making most of psychology all about "repairing" mental "damage" (broken relationships, depressive thoughts, post-traumatic stress, etc.). This is not really a criticism of mainstream psychology. Wanting to help people who are suffering is a worthy calling. Positive psychologists simply argue that there is more to life than dysfunction.

The goal of positive psychology is not to replace mainstream psychology's emphasis on dysfunction, but to expand the field to include the healthy aspects of psychological functioning that help make people happier and mentally stronger. Positive psychology is not a "school" of psychology like Behaviorism or Freudianism, but instead should be considered an "umbrella term" under which may be found a diverse set of researchers and practitioners giving thought to the psychological aspects of "the good life."

Positive psychologists focus their research on positive subjective experiences, positive social organizations, and positive personality traits. Research into personality traits by positive psychologists is the aspect of this movement that has the greatest relevance for our examination of the warrior virtues. Positive psychologists examine character strengths: the impact of these strengths on people's lives, how these strengths may be developed, and what environmental factors help or hinder their development.

A tremendous step forward in the psychological study of positive character traits is the publication of *Character Strengths and Virtues: A Handbook and Classification*,[4] referred to within positive psychological circles as "the CSV." The CSV is based on extensive study of the psychological, philosophical, historical, cross-cultural, educational, and religious literature on the virtues, and it provides an outstanding summary of research and applications in this area. The CSV represents some of the best work currently available involving psychological approaches to the virtues, and has had a powerful impact on my approach to the virtues in this book.[5]

Psychology and the Martial Arts

Very little psychological research has been conducted on the martial arts (I'm hoping to do something about that). However, those few studies that have been done present us with some valuable insights that may be applied to this consideration of the martial virtues, and the role of martial training in character development. In light of the research evidence, examples of which will be discussed below, some psychotherapists have included training in the martial arts as adjuncts to their traditional psychotherapeutic techniques. Others have taken some martial ideas and applied them to the therapeutic process, and martial training has been proposed as a way of encouraging the reform of delinquent youth.

---

4. Christopher Peterson and Martin Seligman, *Character Strengths and Virtues: A Handbook and Classification* (Washington, DC: American Psychological Association, 2004).

5. For those who want to learn more about positive psychology, in addition to the CSV I recommend Christopher Peterson's *Primer in Positive Psychology* (2006, Oxford University Press), the *Handbook of Positive Psychology*, edited by C. R. Snyder and Shane Lopez (2005, Oxford University Press), *A Psychology of Human Strengths*, edited by Lisa Aspinwall and Ursula Staudinger (2003, American Psychological Association), and the articles on positive psychology in the January 2000 special issue of *American Psychologist*.

Several studies have associated martial arts training with reductions in negative characteristics such as anxiety, neuroticism, feelings of vulnerability, and nightmares. This relationship has been demonstrated in studies that are both correlational and experimental in nature.

Other research evidence shows the martial arts also appear to be helpful in the development of positive characteristics. In one study, 60 middle-school boys, who had been identified as being at high risk for delinquency and violence, were assigned to a 10-week Kempo-based school program. Effects of the intervention indicated improvement across 12 different variables, including happiness, attentive ability, and schoolwork performance.

Another researcher's findings resulted in a description of the "superior" martial artist as "an outgoing extrovert somewhat aware of his social environment, looking at himself positively, and trying to get ahead in life." This description lines up with another study of Taekwondo practitioners' personalities, in which the researchers concluded that "belt rank is associated with a pattern of enthusiastic optimism and self-reliance." Martial arts training has also been associated with increases in positive self-image and the ability to tolerate pain.

The relationship between martial arts training and aggressiveness is a contentious one in the psychological literature. The eminent founder of social learning theory, Albert Bandura, argued against the value of martial training in his classic book on aggression. Social learning theory is based on analyzing learned habits of behavior. Habits are learned by experiencing the rewards and punishments associated with the behavior, and by observing the rewards and punishments experienced by others. Aggressive behavior, like other habits of behavior, is learned by being rewarded for aggression and by watching others being rewarded for aggression. The solution to human violence, Bandura argues, is to stop rewarding violent behaviors.

From this perspective, the martial arts are a part of the problem, not the solution. Bandura argues that martial training increases people's aggressiveness by rewarding violent behavior and by providing opportunities to observe others being rewarded for violent behavior. Any talk about a morally defensible form of violent behavior, according to Bandura, is nothing more than a self-justifying façade.

Contrary to Bandura's theorizing, however, the empirical research on martial training paints a different picture. Length of training and higher belt rank is associated with lower aggression and hostility scores in a variety of martial arts, including Karate, Taekwondo, and Jiu Jitsu.

Numerous explanations have been put forward for this demonstrated relationship. Sociologist Terry Nosanchuk argues that the teachings found within the martial arts encourage conflict avoidance, self-control, and respect for others. While sparring involves some degree of violent contact, an overly aggressive fighting style is strongly condemned. Rewarding these patterns of behavior, the author argues, may counteract the pro-violence learning predicted by Bandura. Other researchers claim that martial arts training programs teach values such as respectful kindness, altruism, overcoming fear, and self-control in the face of provocation, and that these values restrain violent impulses.

Having concluded our very brief overview of philosophical and psychological approaches to character, we now turn to the specific question of warrior virtues. Numerous lists of virtues have been produced over the centuries; are there any character strengths that play an especially strong role in a warrior's life? In the next chapter, we begin to address this question.

3

Approaches to the Warrior Virtues

A warrior is a man of action, guided by reason
and motivated by love.

Jack Hoban

Vincite virtute vera.
Conquer by means of virtue.

Plautus

I am a warrior. Not a murderer.

Worf, Son of Mogh

When working within the virtue perspective, the issue immediately arises: which virtues? As scholars throughout the centuries have explored the question of good character, they have produced different lists of virtues that they considered to be essential. So, if the goal of this project is to examine the virtues that constitute an excellent warrior, from where shall we draw *our* list? Plato? Aquinas? The knights of the Round Table? Klingons?

As we saw in the previous chapter, when attempting to develop a list of virtues, the question involves the overall *telos*, or purpose, of humanity, and the virtues that enable people in general to flourish by cultivating those virtues. In our inquiry, the focus is on the lower-level *telos* of a specific practice, the martial arts.

While the overall human *telos* involves the ultimate form of life for all of humanity, the *telos* of a specific practice provides a vision of the ultimate form of excellence as a practitioner of the activity. That vision establishes a standard by which practitioners can be evaluated, and a description of the virtues that make someone the perfect practitioner.[6] In this case, the topic at hand is specifically the virtues that enable a warrior to flourish *as a warrior*. The *telos* that informs this project, then, is that of a perfect warrior. If we set a vision of the perfect warrior as our standard, we are able to use that standard to evaluate ourselves and to guide our training.

So how do we describe the perfect warrior? Several texts, some of them historical treatises and some of them recent scholarly works on warriorhood, were examined in the attempt to assemble a list of virtues that are considered essential to the practice of the martial arts.

Western Warriors: Martial Virtues in Greece, Rome, Europe, and America

Heroic Virtues in Homer, Plato, and Virgil

Thus proclaim I, and it shall be accomplished: I will utterly bruise mine adversary's flesh and break his bones, so let his friends abide together here to bear him forth when vanquished by my hands.

Iliad, chapter XXIII

The *Iliad*, Homer's 7th-century BCE epic poem, is set during the Trojan War. Like so many conflicts, the central problem of the

---

6. At this level of analysis, MacIntyre's definition of a virtue is: "an acquired human quality the possession and exercise of which tends to enable us to achieve those goods which are internal to practices and the lack of which effectively prevents us from achieving any such goods." (After Virtue, page 191.)

Trojan War is two men fighting over the same woman. Helen, the wife of the Spartan king Menelaus, was carried off by the Trojan prince Paris (reports are unclear as to whether she was kidnapped or ran away with Paris). To get her back took ten years, and cost the lives of many great warriors. In one particular passage of the *Iliad*, the young warrior Glaukos boasts of his heroic background. In doing so, he provides what one classical scholar calls a "perfect summary of most of the nuances implicit in the ideal of *aretê* [virtue] in its Homeric context." The portrait that emerges from Glaukos' autobiographical passage describes

> "a kindly hero whose *aretê* is defined in terms of his noble birth and origin, his bodily strength and beauty, his valor and courage, his ability to do what others cannot; or in terms of his glory and honor, his power and wealth, his youthful forcefulness, his skillfulness of body and mind, his intelligence and craftiness, his resourcefulness and wisdom."

This description may be condensed by combining roughly-synonymous virtues, resulting in a Homeric hero who is characterized by (1) high social standing, (2) strength, (3) beauty, (4) courage, (5) skill, and (6) practical wisdom. Some of the traits listed here may strike readers as odd. The modern mind is used to the word "virtue" primarily referring to moral qualities, and traits such as physical strength, beauty, and high social status are typically considered morally neutral. Remember, though, that the word "virtue" in this context refers to any characteristic that enables an individual to better fulfill the *telos*. Homer's description of an ideal warrior makes no distinction between "internal" (psychological) and "external" (physical/environmental) characteristics, and fits well in a Greek approach to the virtues.

Although Glaukos' speech provides academics with a good look at Homeric virtues, and Achilles is the character in the *Iliad* who demonstrates the greatest lethality in battle, the character that best shows a noble spirit is Hector. Hector, brother of the homewrecking Paris, shows his noble character several times in the epic. He criticizes Paris for cowardice and selfishness, starting a war over Helen and then refusing to fight in it. His single combat with Ajax is so impressive that the fight ends with mutual admiration and friendship rather than hatred, and the two combatants exchange gifts. When death finally comes to Hector, he faces it with fatalism, resolved to meet his end with bravery. Hector's display of virtue has resulted in millennia of warriors looking to him as a role model. During the medieval period, he was listed among the Nine Worthies, great warriors whose lives were held up as examples for students of chivalry.

Written around 390 BCE, Plato's *Republic* is a masterwork of ancient Greek philosophy. In it, the question is asked: "What is justice?" Developing the answer to that question takes the reader through platonic thought on such topics as politics, ethics, psychology, education, and war.

Although discussion of Plato and the virtues typically centers around his four Cardinal Virtues (wisdom, justice, courage, and temperance) described in Book V of *The Republic*, a section in Book II contains a discussion of the ideal qualities for one who fulfills the role of "guardian" (the warrior class of Plato's ideal society). In this discussion, the qualities of an ideal warrior are compared to the qualities necessary for an ideal guard dog (not the most flattering approach, but one that many warriors embrace). The ideal guard dog, Plato argues, must be fast, strong, courageous, intelligent enough to know friend from foe, and gentle to those whom he is protecting. In the same way, Plato lists the ideal virtues of the guardian as speed, strength, "high spirits" (the aggressive vitality that is necessary for courage), and a "philosophic disposition" (a virtue which Plato claims incorporates both the wisdom of knowing enemy from ally, and the gentleness that enables a guardian to lay down his life for his neighbors).

Moving from Greek thought to Roman, in the *Aeneid*, Virgil's 1st-century BCE epic, the character Aeneas is a hero of the Trojan War, who eventually founds the city of Rome. Comparing Homer's and Virgil's warriors, classicist Carol Andreini puts forward the idea that the problem with the central heroes of the *Iliad*

(Achilles and Hector) is that they do not reach beyond the roles of their immediate social context (soldier, son, husband, etc.), and that this is reflected in the nature of their virtues.

By requiring his hero to operate in a larger world, Virgil's Aeneas becomes a warrior of overall high character. "Achilles is best suited to success in war, Aeneas to responsibility in general." The key virtue that distinguishes Aeneas from Achilles is piety, which Andreini describes as the quality of being "devoted," "true-hearted," or "duty-bound."

German philosopher Josef Pieper regards piety as a form of justice, in which the individual gives "that which is due" to something larger than themselves. A pious citizen gives the state the support and obedience to which it is due. An example of piety in monotheistic religion would be giving God "the glory due his name" (Psalm 29:2) through acts of reverence and worship. Filial piety requires that children respect and honor their parents.

Far from being merely one more virtue tacked onto the list, piety transforms and directs the other warrior virtues, orienting heroic activity toward worthier goals than personal glory. We will discuss piety and its role in the life of a warrior in some depth in the chapter devoted to justice. Andreini asserts that "it is only when the heroism of the warrior is combined with *pietas* [piety] and works for a goal other than individual glory—be it for the country, the family, the gods—that anything is truly won."

Chivalry: Virtues of the Christian Knight

For on being converted to the Lord, from being free men of iniquity they became the slaves of justice, and they exert themselves to please God first and then, because of God, men, working for the welfare of their brothers instead of their own, loving God, above all things, and their neighbor, laying down their bodies under another master.

The Rule of the Spanish Military Order of St James

In 12th-century England, a lad by the name of William was clearly not destined for greatness. The fourth son of a minor noble, William's father did not even consider him valuable as a hostage; when King Stephen besieged their castle and threatened to hang William if his father did not surrender, William's father dared the king to kill the child. Fortunately, King Stephen was feeling merciful. At age 21, William was serving as a squire to his father's cousin. As a squire, William's primary skills appeared to involve eating and sleeping, but when he was knighted and sent into battle in 1167, William showed himself to be a formidable warrior. He then went on to compete in the tournaments, impressing onlookers with his strength and skill. William reportedly won 500 tournament bouts, never once losing.

From his unimpressive beginnings, William rose to prominence through his martial ability and repeated demonstrations of courage and loyalty. In 1170, King Henry II appointed William to be his son's tutor in chivalry. For twelve years, William taught the young man the handling of weapons, taught him the martial virtues, and also served as his bodyguard. Although the two fell out, before the prince died at age 28 he reconciled with William and asked him to crusade in his name. After fighting alongside the Templars for three years, William returned to England and served in the courts of four successive Plantagenet kings. He was a lover of battle and of honor, and he believed that the two should go hand in hand.

One incident in particular demonstrates these two qualities in William's life. In 1189, King Henry's son Richard took advantage of Henry's illness to attempt a coup. William encountered Richard in a rare moment of vulnerability, and charged at him. It would have been entirely understandable for William to kill the rebellious Richard, but even a rebelling member of the Plantagenet family is still a member of that family. William's loyalty to the royal family was so strong that he redirected his lance thrust, killing Richard's horse but sparing his life. Richard begged for mercy, and William granted it. When Henry died, William was retained as an honored regent of the new ruler, known to history as the warrior king Richard the Lionheart. Wiliam's loyalty never wavered, and his courage never failed. He has been called the "flower of chivalry," and "the greatest knight that ever lived."

Historian Maurice Keen describes the ethic of chivalry as a fusion of martial, aristocratic, and Christian values. While nobility was associated with the upper classes (especially considering the tremendous cost of purchasing and maintaining the necessary equipment such as horse and armor), high birth did not necessarily guarantee chivalric glory, and low birth could be overcome by sufficient demonstrations of worth. Nobility, therefore, could be associated with having worthy character as much as having the right parents. Arthurian legends supported this meritocratic ideal, with Arthur's round table serving as "an emblem of the equal terms on which all knights, great and humble, mixed at his board once they had, by prowess or service, won their right to a place there."

Medieval literature, often centering around the Arthur legend, was one of the major inspirations for chivalry. The stories held up legendary and historical warriors as prototypes worthy of study (especially popular were the "Nine Worthies": Joshua, King David, Judas Maccabeus, Hector, Alexander the Great, Julius Caesar, King Arthur, Charlemagne, and Godfrey de Bullion). Theologians and philosophers also wrote treatises on the proper role of the military in society, and many instructional manuals were published for the training of young knights. Examining the literature produced during this period, Keen lists the "classic virtues of good knighthood" as prowess, loyalty, generosity, courtesy, and *franchise*. Keen defines *franchise* as "the free and frank bearing that is visible testimony to the combination of good birth with virtue," and as the "independent spirit" of the gentleman. Malcolm Vale, on the other hand, considers *franchise* to be "integrity." Taken together, the description of *franchise* that we see is one in which one's outward behavior lines up with one's true inner worth.

In his book *War and Chivalry*, historian Malcolm Vale examines two of the aforementioned "instructional manuals" designed to guide young warriors in their preparation for heroic acts. Two fifteenth-century documents (*L'Instruction d'un Jeune Prince* and *Enseignment de Vraie Noblesse*) list the four platonic Cardinal Virtues (wisdom, justice, courage, and temperance) as the virtues characteristic of an ideal knight. One interesting thing about these manuscripts is that, unlike most approaches to the Cardinal Virtues, courage rather than wisdom is described as the supreme virtue. Without the courage to act, nothing of worth is accomplished.

When examining the interaction of knighthood and Christianity, a topic of particular relevance is the establishment of the "military orders." In the wake of the First Crusade, the city of Jerusalem was in European hands, opening wide opportunities for trade and religious pilgrimage. However, the roads that ran through the areas were largely uncontrolled, and travelers were under constant threat of ambush and robbery.

The 12th-century chronicles of William, Archbishop of Tyre, indicate that in the year 1118, "pious and God-fearing" knights (Hugh of Payns and Godfrey of Saint-Omer being the most prominent) took monastic vows at the hands of Warmund of Piquigny, Patriarch of Jerusalem. This is the founding of the Knights of the Order of the Temple of Solomon, known popularly as the Templars. The Templars were granted resources, and charged with protecting the roads and highways for the safety of travelers to and from Jerusalem. Two decades later, Pope Innocent II gave the Templars the official sanction of the Church. They were to be knights of Christ.

After the formation of the Templar order, the Order of the Hospital of Saint John, dedicated to providing shelter and medical attention to travelers, expanded their operations to include military protection. These military orders, and others founded during that century,[7] drew from the Templar example, attempting to establish the ideal of a warrior-monk who fought exclusively for the protection of the weak, the upholding of justice, and the service of God. The Templars operated for almost two centuries. In 1312, facing the combined opposition of Pope Clement V and King Philip IV of France, the Templars were suppressed amid public scandal and accusations of moral corruption. Medieval historian Sophia Menache sees the public outrage over the accusations against the Templars as a reflection of the lofty moral ideals to which they had aspired. Like many who are held up as public examples of righteousness, having aimed high, they had farther to fall.

The Templars' ethical ideal was laid out by Bernard of Clairveaux, a Cistercian monk who met with Hugh of Payns in 1127. Greatly impressed with these knights of Christ, he penned *De Laude Novae Militae* ("In Praise of the New Knighthood") around 1130, in which he describes the Templars as "both more gentle than lambs, and more ferocious than lions, that I almost doubt what I prefer them to be called, namely monks or knights, unless I should call them in fact most suitably by both, in whom neither is known to be lacking, neither the gentleness of the monk nor the strength of the knight."

The monastic vows of the Templars were poverty, chastity, and obedience. Rather than considering these three vows as virtues in and of themselves, the 14th-century *Rule of the Spanish Military Order of St. James* describes the vows of these warrior-monks as "established as fulfillment of the true and perfect charity." Thomas Aquinas considered charity (sacrificial love) to be supreme among Christian virtues.

Chivalry was "an attempt to tame murderous instincts by providing a Christian ideal of the warrior." In doing so, the excessive brutality of war could be curbed, military force could be held to

---

7. Examples include the Order of Saint Lazarus in 1130, the Spanish Order of Saint James in 1170, and the Teutonic Knights in 1198.

an expectation of defending the weak instead of acting in simple self-centered ambition, and the individual warrior could find a way of personal spiritual growth that was coherent with his role in battle.

The heyday of chivalry was roughly between 1100 and 1500. After that, innovations in the chivalric ideal dwindled, and it began to lose its place as Europe's dominant ethical ideal.

Chivalry did, however, continue (and still does continue) to influence Western civilization's notions of personal morality and honorable behavior. The connection between martial training and virtues of character had a profound influence on Renaissance and Reformation educational theory (Reformers such as Martin Luther and Ulrich Zwingli supported the idea that exercise in jousting, fencing, and wrestling should be employed to promote moral health). The late-sixteenth-century English defense master George Silver, for example, claimed that training in the arts of defense produces a wealth of benefits, physical, emotional, cognitive, and moral. Nineteenth-century scholar Richard F. Burton connected the chivalric ideal to American notions of honor and heroism, an idea reflected in Mark Twain's satirical comment that the Civil War was fought because Southerners read too many of Sir Walter Scott's medieval novels.

Fiore dei Liberi's Bestiary

So he also lacks all who lacks audacity of the heart;
Audacity is the virtue that makes this art.

Fiore dei Liberi

Fiore dei Liberi, in the prologue of his treatise, *Flos Duellatorum* ("Flower of Battle"), describes his early life in the small town of Cividale. Wishing to learn swordsmanship from the best instructors available, he left the northern Italian village of his birth. In his travels, he trained under numerous German and Italian masters of defense, the most prominent being Johannes Suvenus. After two decades of experience as a soldier and duelist, he eventually entered the court of Niccolo III d'Este, the Marquis of Ferrara, where he acquired a commission in the early 1400s as a master swordsman. He then began to write his manuscript, which he completed in 1410, in which he describes the techniques central to his martial system. Current students of medieval European martial arts often look to *Flos Duellatorum* as a guide and training manual, and many consider it to be without equal among pre-Renaissance manuscripts on the arts of defense.

The essence of Liberi's art is symbolized in an illustration found in *Flos Duellatorum,* and in it Liberi lists and describes virtues of an excellent practitioner of his art. The illustration features the image of a man with seven swords superimposed over his body, indicating the seven angles of attack, and the images of four animals, representing four "metaphysical attributes" of a master swordsman. These four metaphysical attributes may be considered Liberi's list of martial virtues. The four animals and their corresponding virtues are as follows: at the top of the illustration sits a lynx holding a compass, with the word *prudentia* (prudence). To the left of the image is the figure of a lion holding a heart, with the word *audatia* (courage/audacity). To the right sits a tiger holding an arrow, with the word *celeritas* (swiftness). At the bottom of the illustration stands an elephant bearing a castle on its back, with the word *fortitudo* (strength). The ideal fighter in Liberi's system balances all four virtues.

North American Images of the Hero

You know what you get for being a hero? Nothin'. You get shot at. You get a little pat on the back, blah, blah, blah, attaboy. You get divorced. Your wife can't remember your last name. Your kids don't want to talk to you. You get to eat a lot of meals by yourself. Trust me, kid, nobody wants to be that guy.
Then why do you do it?
Because there's nobody else to do it, that's why.
                    Live Free or Die Hard (20th Century Fox, 2007)

As we have seen in Homer, Virgil, and the chivalric literature, you can learn a lot about how a culture views heroism by looking at the stories they tell. What about our own culture? In his 1994 book *Warrior Dreams*, anthropologist John Donahue examines the mythology of heroism within American culture, and connects this image to the martial arts. Examining elements of North American cinema, he finds three central elements to the makeup of a hero in the American mind. Whether the hero is a gunslinging cowboy, a wisecracking private detective, a commando operating behind enemy lines, a hardened cop, or the last of the Jedi, the hero is (1) skillful in violence, (2) socially marginalized, and (3) morally correct in motivation.

. Donahue connects these elements of the hero to the American ideal of rugged individualism. Americans often struggle with the conflicting values of individualism and community. The action hero achieves both. He is connected to a larger community in his role of protector/avenger, and it is from that source that he gains his moral authority to engage in violent behavior. But violence is generally outside of the norms of society, so the hero becomes a loner. The hero's status as a rogue is then transformed from a liability into a virtue, as the hero's self-reliance allows him to act independently to defeat the villain and protect the community.

In standard cinematic fare (and this may be extended to other forms of media), the villain shares the first two characteristics of martial prowess and social marginality. Chong Li, the villain of the movie *Bloodsport*, is shown as marginalized when he is shunned by tournament authorities for killing an opponent in a match. Ivan Drago, the Russian boxer in *Rocky IV,* is portrayed as a mere tool of his Soviet superiors, to the degree that his own wife appears to be nothing more than his handler and spokeswoman. Even if the villain does exist in a community, that community is relegated to the status of an out-group. Johnny, the evil student who bullied *The Karate Kid*, may be connected to the local wealthy society, but that society is portrayed as elitist and morally inferior to the hero's blue-collar apartment complex. The villainous commandos-turned-criminals in *Lethal Weapon* are loyal members of a tight-knit cadre, but it is a cadre of drug dealers (whom even other drug dealers find off-putting).

It is the element of justice that separates the hero from the villain. Even Sam Spade, the apparently amoral "anti-hero" of *The Maltese Falcon*, characterized by ruthlessness, cynicism, adultery, and callousness, passes up the prospect of financial gain and (maybe) love because of the rough morality that you are "supposed to do something about it" if your partner is murdered. This kind of minimalist case is the exception, but such cases do demonstrate that justice is the central virtue of the North American hero.

Philosopher Sandrine Berges, in her analysis of "hardboiled detectives" like Sam Spade, add practical wisdom to the list, pointing out that the hero's operations outside of mainstream society requires the hero to act without the guidance of the rules of mainstream society. Instead, the detective must rely on on-the-spot problem-solving skills in rapidly changing environments, a form of information processing that is central to practical wisdom.

Eastern Warriors: Virtues within Asian Ethical Thought

While Western notions of the virtuous warrior are primarily influenced by the integration of classical philosophy and Christian theology, Asian martial culture primarily resulted from some form of interaction between Buddhism, Taoism, and Confucianism.

In some cases, all three contributed to the vision of the perfect warrior (an example being the Korean hwarang). In other cases, Buddhist detachment and Taoist naturalism combined to reject Confucian concepts of propriety,[8] while in other cases, it was Buddhism that was downplayed (an example being Tsunetomo's comments in *Hagakure* that young samurai should avoid too much Buddhism, leaving that system of thought to the el-

---

8. Order of Shaolin Ch'an, *The Shaolin Grandmasters' Text: History, Philosophy and Gung Fu of Shaolin Ch'an* (Beaverton, OR: Tuttle Publishing, 2004).

derly). But even in cases in which one of these systems of thought is rejected, the warrior's reaction against the rejected tradition was itself a (negative) factor in the combined effect of all three in shaping the Asian image of the ideal martial artist.

Confucian Virtues

If there be righteousness in the heart,
there will be beauty in the character,
If there be beauty in the character,
there will be harmony in the home.
If there be harmony in the home,
there will be order in the nation.
If there be order in the nation,
there will be peace in the world.

Book of Rites

The Confucian martial artist is both warrior and scholar. Beginning with the writings of Confucius (551-479 BCE), and developed through subsequent work by scholars such as Mencius (372-289 BCE) and Zhu Xi (1130-1200 AD), Confucian thought on character development aims at cultivating the self, with the goal of producing an individual of *ren*[9], an overarching "master virtue" described by Slingerland as the quality of being "truly human." Possible translations of *ren* include "humaneness," "benevolence," or "humanity." Work done within the Confucian stream of thought have had a tremendous and wide-ranging impact on the Asian martial arts (For example, William Bodiford argues that about 80% of traditional Japanese martial training is based on neo-Confucian self-cultivation concepts).

The Five Constant Virtues of Confucian ethics are benevolence, righteousness, courteousness, wisdom, and honesty. Training in these virtues involves study, especially of classic literature, and the continuous practice of rituals covering the proper meth-

---

9. Some scholars transliterate "ren" as "jen."

od for social behaviors ranging from the wearing of clothes to the receiving of gifts. The repetition of precise behaviors in the proper manner is intended to internalize the principles of correct action, thought, and emotion. As mastery of these principles grows, the student slowly gains a degree of flexibility, and eventually autonomy from the specific rules. The sage knows how and when to apply the rules of behavior in a given context, to the degree that the rules may even be technically broken when the situation calls for it.

Students of the martial arts will immediately recognize these principles, as they may be applied to the use of *kata* (forms) in training. The student begins by doing kata in a mechanistic "by the book" manner. After extensive repetition, the student begins to internalize the principles "behind" the form. Once the principle has been internalized, the student gains the flexibility to spontaneously adapt the form to specific situations, to the degree that novices who observe the expert may think that the expert is "violating" the form. In the words of Bujinkan Grandmaster Masaaki Hatsumi: "It is not about studying a technique. It is about looking for something deeper underlying the techniques."

Buddhist Virtues

A monk cannot fulfill the Buddhist Way if he does not manifest compassion without and persistently store up courage within. And if a warrior does not manifest courage without and hold enough compassion within his heart to burst his chest, he cannot become a retainer. Therefore the monk pursues courage with the warrior as his model, and the warrior pursues the compassion of the monk.

Hagakure

The First Noble Truth of Buddhism is that life is suffering. The Second is that the cause of life's suffering can be traced to attachment: to possessions, to people, to ideas, to situations, to self. The heart of Buddhist ethics is the alleviation of suffering, and this is accomplished through methods that are aimed at liberating people from attachments. Methods of cultivating the necessary detachment include the Threefold Training of study, instruction, and practice. Study and instruction assist students in learning that all reality is actually one, and that perceptions of separate entities (including one's own existence as an individual) is illusion. This realization is the core of Buddhist wisdom. Practices that assist in detachment from illusions of individual separateness include meditation, self-reflexive "savoring," and mindfulness training.

Damien Keown lists three "Buddhist Cardinal Virtues": liberality, benevolence, and understanding, virtues that may be developed through meditation and the contemplation of Buddhist concepts. He describes Buddhist ethics as purposeful in nature, as the goal of these endeavors is to cultivate the person toward the ideal state of nirvana, described by Keown as perfection in both moral and intellectual terms.

In his examination of the Theravada stream of Buddhist thought, Donald Swearer makes the claim that Buddhism's "ten moral perfections" (renunciation, endeavor, loving-kindness, determination, wisdom, good conduct, forbearance, equanimity, truthfulness, and generosity) can be conceptually condensed into two virtues: benevolence and self-renunciation. These two virtues are found in the Mahayana stream of Buddhist thought, as well.

By detaching from the illusion of individual existence, one recognizes that there is no real self/not-self division, and therefore no separation between oneself and other people. Detachment from self is therefore the basis of Buddhist benevolence, as one is motivated to be "equally friendly to oneself, friends, strangers, and enemies." E. A. Burtt describes the Buddha's love as "no dependent attachment to a person or object through whom one hopes to find his longings satisfied, but an unlimited self-giving compassion flowing freely toward all creatures that live."

Taoism: Virtues of the Way

We do not see its form
We do not hear its sound
Yet we can perceive an order to its accomplishments
We call it "the Way.

Nei-Yeh

Studies of Taoism typically center around three fundamental texts: the *Tao Te Ching*, the *Nan Hua Ching*, and the *Nei-Yeh*. These three texts were assembled some time in the 3rd or 4th centuries BCE, and they reflect a school of thought that features the idea that there is a fundamental unity to the universe (the "Tao" is the "Way" of the universe), and that the perfect person (*chen-jen*) lives in harmony with that order.

Behavior in harmony with the Tao is characterized by *wu wei*, translated as "inaction" or "non-assertive action" that promotes, rather than disrupts, harmony with the Tao ("The way of the Tao is to yield." *Tao Te Ching*, Verse 40). Harmony with the Tao is characterized by balance, illustrated by the "*taiji*," the swirling yin-yang symbol familiar to almost all martial artists. By living in harmony with the universe, the person is able to transcend the mortal condition, facing life with selfless morality, and facing death with peace. Selflessness in Taoism is motivated by an understanding that we all exist as inseparable parts of the universe. Behavior in harmony with the Tao is also characterized by *ziran*, a virtue often translated as "spontaneity," as the Tao has no origin other than itself. A life of *ziran* is stripped of artifice, characterized by authenticity, and relatively free of effort.

Selfless, effortless, non-assertive action is seen in the *Tao Te Ching*'s description of a great ruler:

> The great ruler speaks little
> and his words are priceless
> He works without self-interest
> and leaves no trace

When all is finished, the people say,
"It happened by itself." (Verse 17)

Approaching Taoism from a virtue perspective, researchers associated with the positive psychology movement describe *ziran* to be the "master" virtue of Taoism, while other scholars give that place to harmony or balance. Herman Kauz, commenting on the connection between Taoism and the practice of the martial arts, identifies principles that could be interpreted along virtue lines, including respect for life and nature, non-action, moderation, filial piety, and enlightenment.

Taoist concepts are ubiquitous in Asian martial arts, influencing styles that are widely divergent in method and approach. The Taoist principle of harmonious yielding, for example, is applied to combat in verse 31 of the *Tao Te Ching*: "Even the finest warrior is defeated when he goes against natural law". In Aikido, this is translated into the foundational concept of *muteiko* (non-resistance). This principle is also found in the ninpo writings of Masaaki Hatsumi: "Do not search for victory or seek gain, allow it to happen naturally: just as flint and steel come together to make fire." This ubiquity exists to such a degree that one scholar makes the claim that, if anyone is a practitioner of an Asian martial art (particularly one with the word "do" in the name, such as Judo or Hapkido), that person is, by default, a Taoist.

Warrior Virtues in the Asian Martial Arts: China, Korea, and Japan

China

Examining Chinese warrior culture, James Liu's book *The Chinese Knight-Errant* targets a group of wandering fighters referred to as *yu-hsia*. Comparing them (in some aspects) to their knightly European counterparts, the *yu-hsia* were typically nobles who had fallen on hard times, or peasants turned professional warriors.

Liu is quick to point out, though, that these were not amoral mercenaries, but wandering adventurers who often possessed strong moral characteristics. "The essential qualifications of a knight errant were not so much outstanding physical strength and military skill as a spirit of altruism and a concern for justice. In short, knight errantry was not a profession but a way of behaviour, and a knight errant was simply a man who sought to right wrongs and help people in distress, often by the use of force and in defiance of the law."

In contrast to stereotypes that many have of Asian society, these warriors were individualists. Rejecting Confucian conformist principles, the ethic of the *yu-hsia* preferred loyalty to one's friends and one's personal sense of justice over the fulfillment of a social role (This places the *yu-hsia* in direct contrast with the samurai's idea of loyalty, which was explicitly attached to the warrior's lord).

One famous "knight-errant" was Kuo Chieh. Growing from a wild and angry young man into more virtuous adulthood, Kuo was a second-century BCE Chinese Robin Hood. He robbed from the rich, helped his friends who were in trouble with the law, and avenged wrongs, all at the risk of his own life and with no thought of fortune or glory. When Kuo's nephew engaged in some shenanigans that resulted in another man killing him, Kuo tracked down the killer. But when Kuo found out what had happened, he refused to take revenge, valuing justice even over family. Kuo was so inspiring to those around him that, when he refused to take revenge for his own sake, others would secretly do it for him.

Liu considers the *yu-hsia*'s ethic to show "more affinity with Taoism than with any other school of thought" due to the parallels between their individualistic freedom and Taoist authenticity. The *yu-hsia* tradition also provides a fertile ground for female warriors.

A story, set in the T'ang Dynasty (7th through 10th century AD), is told of a woman named Hung Hsien. Hung Hsien worked for a regional governor, who was having problems with a rival governor. As the rival prepared to invade, Hung Hsien pulled her hair back into a bun and disappeared into the night, armed only with a small dagger. She snuck into the rival's headquarters and stole a gold case from his bedside. When she returned, she gave the case to her employer, who had it delivered back to the rival as a not-so-subtle threat. The rival immediately cancelled the invasion. Like many of the great heroic characters, Hung Hsien politely said goodbye and departed, never to be seen again.

Liu describes the virtues held dear by the *yu-hsia* as altruism, justice, individual freedom, personal loyalty, courage, truthfulness, honor, and generosity. References to *yu-hsia* first appeared during China's Warring States period (403-221 BCE), and numerous stories were told of their exploits. A renewed interest in Confucian thought among China's rulers led to a suppression of the *yu-hsia* during the Han dynasty (beginning around the second century BCE), after which this type of warrior dwindled from the historical scene, though not quite disappearing until the mid 19th century. The *yu-hsia* continue to influence Chinese ideas of martial heroism as main characters in the *wuxia* genre of literature and cinema (the Academy Award-winning Ang Lee movie *Crouching Tiger, Hidden Dragon* serves as an example).

Representing a different Chinese tradition, the Gung Fu practitioners of the Shaolin Ch'an Order see their training in the martial arts primarily as a vehicle for spiritual development: "Shaolin are Buddhists first and martial artists second, or third."

The Mahayana ideals of the Shaolin reflect the virtues of benevolence and enlightened self-renunciation: "The most important things a person can do in a lifetime, then, are to acknowledge kinship with all sentient life and to eliminate ego and the causes of attachment."

Tid Kiu Sam, a nineteenth-century disciple of the Shaolin monk Gwok Yan, is revered among practitioners of southern Gung Fu, many of whom continue to practice his "Tid Sin Kuen" training form. In addition to his phenomenal strength, Tid Kiu Sam was known for his humility and wisdom. Early in his career, he was challenged by a renowned Gung Fu master. He tried to politely decline, but the ego of his challenger would not permit it. Tid Kiu Sam won the match, and his opponent attempted to get revenge by preparing an ambush. His ability to size up a situation allowed Tid Kiu Sam to see through the trap and avoid it. Tid Kiu Sam's strength, skill, and wisdom were known far and wide, and he is honored to this day as one of the "Ten Tigers of Guangdong."

Korea

Although the technical aspects of modern martial Korean arts such as Taekwondo, Hapkido, and Tangsoodo are derived from Chinese and Japanese fighting styles, Korean martial artists typically trace the moral components of their system to the hwarang, an aristocratic society, dedicated to warrior ideals, that lasted from the sixth to eighth centuries AD in the ancient Korean kingdom of Silla.

Hwarang came from the elite of Silla society, and were chosen for their physical beauty as well as their warrior prowess. It was said that there was no greater honor for a Sillan family than to have a son who became a hwarang and gave his life in the service of his country. Historian Vladimir Tikhonov describes the essence of hwarang morality as the ability "to be psychologically able to dispose of one's life whenever it was deemed necessary." The virtues considered necessary for this process were "mercifulness toward living creatures, indifference to material temptations, and, most importantly, a calm and optimistic attitude toward death." In the early seventh century, the Buddhist monk Wongwang provided the hwarang with Five Commandments to guide them: (1) to be loyal to their lord, (2) to show piety to their parents, (3) to be a trustworthy friend, (4) to never retreat from battle, and (5) to only kill when justice requires it.

One of the most famous historical hwarang was Kim Yu-shin, the Sillan general who was instrumental in the seventh-century unification of the Korean peninsula. Kim Yu-shin was supremely devoted to duty, and stories that are told of his life focus on the extremes to which he would go in the name of what he believed to be right. He sacrificed his love life for the sake of his martial training, was prepared to fight a battle over an unjust accusation, charged alone into an enemy encampment in order to inspire his troops, and disowned his own son in the name of honor.

The ideals of the hwarang continue to influence modern Korean martial arts, many of which incorporate Wongmang's Five Commandments into their curriculum. When the Cuban Taekwondo competitor Angel Matos lost his temper during the 2008 Olympics, kicking a referee, pushing a judge, and spitting on the arena floor, World Taekwondo Federation general secretary Yang Jin-suk called it an insult to the spirit of Taekwondo and an insult to all mankind. For his demonstration of poor character, Matos has been banned for life by the WTF.

Bushido in Japan

In feudal Japan, the ethical component of samurai life was the code of conduct and character that we have come to refer to as *bushido.* Through education in Chinese classic literature (including Confucian works), and fine arts such as poetry and flower arrangement, the samurai was to be a cultivated man of both fierce action and humane refinement. In addition to providing a structure for social relationships and interactions, bushido outlined the proper form of a warrior's character.

Seventeenth-century bushido prodigy Kumazawa Banzan stated that "a good warrior is always courageous and deeply devoted to the way of the warrior and martial arts; he takes care not to stumble no matter what happens, respects his rules, pities [has compassion toward] everyone from his wife and children to the old and young all over the world, and prefers peace in the world from a humane and loving heart."[10]

Some scholars focus on the practical benefits of this system of character formation. Rattti and Westbrook claim that, although

10. Thomas Cleary (Trans.), *Training the Samurai Mind: A Bushido Sourcebook* (Boston: Shambhala Publications), 56.

bushido involved an adaptation of Buddhist self-renunciation as the primary virtue, this self-renunciation did not aim at the attainment of enlightenment, but at the production of the perfectly fearless warrior, able to lay his life down for his lord without hesitation.

In an interview with anthropologist Howard Reid, Master Risuke Otake of the Tenshin Shoden Katori Shinto Ryu tells the story of a samurai by the name of Torisunaemon. In the late 16th century, Takada warriors had surrounded Nagashino Castle, and the Shogun loyalists within were starving to death. Torisunaemon was chosen to escape from the castle and try to get word to the Shogun and request aid. He completed his mission, but was captured as he returned. The commander of the enemy forces offered Torisunaemon a position of prominence in his army if he would only tell the inhabitants of the castle that no help would arrive. Torisunaemon agreed, but when the moment came to deliver the demoralizing message, he instead yelled to the loyalists the true message that help would arrive in a matter of days. The Takada samurai immediately killed Torisunaemon, but he died honorably, sacrificing himself for the sake of his lord.

In his classic book on the subject, Inazo Nitobe's approach to bushido is less cynical than that of Rattti and Westbrook. Nitobe focuses on the ideal of the samurai as a man of great moral rectitude, describing the bushido ethic as the root and flower of all that is beautiful in Japanese culture. Nitobe directly employs the language of virtue when describing the character of the samurai. His discussion of the samurai virtues involves examinations of justice, courage, benevolence, politeness, sincerity, honor, loyalty, and self-control.[11]

Yasaroku Soyeshima combines the idealistic and the pragmatic in his approach to bushido, referring to it as a system of practical morality, the ultimate goal of which was the advancement of "the heaven-ordained mission of the Japanese Empire." By identifying

---

11. Inazo Nitobe, *Bushido: The Soul of Japan.* (Rutland, VT: Charles E. Tuttle Company, 1969, original work 1905).

the rise of Japan to a position of power and glory as the ethical *telos*, the pragmatic benefits of developing fearless warriors and the moral excellence of selfless service are united.

Two elements of Soyeshima's treatment of bushido may be approached from a virtue perspective. First, Soyeshima lists the "Four Vows" of bushido, stating that "Bushido demands (1) Death, (2) Fidelity, (3) Dignity, and (4) Prudence." The notion that bushido demands death is an indicator of the complete selflessness of the samurai, a sentiment repeatedly emphasized in *Hagakure* ("The Way of the Samurai is found in death"). The second relevant element in Soyeshima's work is his "Four Principles" of bushido: (1) to fall behind none in bushido, (2) to be of service to the Master-Lord, (3) to be faithful to one's parents, and (4) to be merciful and self-sacrificing. These principles are also found in *Hagakure*, along with the virtues of intelligence, humanity and courage.

Ninjutsu in Japan

A young man, whose name was Jutaro, was a diligent student of the martial arts. Striken with sickness, he retreated to a secluded area in the wilderness, believing that communion with nature would be the best cure. He lived a simple and ascetic existence, and over time (and with the assistance of a mysterious old man) he recovered and grew stronger than ever. The trees, the rocks, the waterfall, all of them served as his training partners, and he came to understand that a life of wisdom, righteousness, and power came from living according to the principles of nature.

The young man known as Jutaro grew up, and is better known to martial arts scholars as Toshitsugu Takamatsu, 33rd Grandmaster of Togakure Ryu Ninjutsu. The teachings that Takamatsu passed on reflect the idea found in Taoism (and Plato's philosophy) that there is a moral order to nature. There is no difference between operating according to the laws of nature in the way that a fighter moves his body, and the way that a virtuous person interacts with others. Body, intellect, and spirit must all function as nature designed them to function. "I have been training" said

Takamatsu, "believing that martial arts provided a technique to overcome the enemy... But when I think about the proper direction of gaining enlightenment or the nature of such arts, it all boils down to learning the laws of nature."

Takamatsu's pupil, now the 34th Grandmaster of Togakure Ryu Ninjutsu (along with the other eight martial systems that make up the curriculum of the Bujinkan organization), Masaaki Hatsumi is heir to a martial lineage that stretches back to the mid twelfth century. Through his writings, his teachings, his leadership and his life, Hatsumi has endeavored to present the legacy of the ninja to the world.

In opposition to the popular stereotypes of ninjas as thieving mercenaries or as cold-blooded monsters, Hatsumi maintains that the philosophical outlook (referred to as *ninpo*) held by the ninja families is one of enlightened service. In history's many conflicts, the side with money and power will field large armies to accomplish its goals, while the smaller and less powerful have to make use of guerilla tactics, sabotage, and assassination. And so it was in Japan.

The philosophy of ninpo stands as a counterpart to the approach to life and morality found in bushido. In contrast to the samurai's emphasis on highly public displays of loyalty and courage, ninja were required to work in secret. In order to maintain a stable sense of self while employing disguise and deception, ninpo emphasizes the internal aspects of honorable living. An examination of several of Hatsumi's books indicates a recurring endorsement of the following virtues: devotion to family and country, perseverance, harmony with nature, self-control, spontaneity, *kyojitsu tenkan ho* (a complex virtue that involves an understanding of truth and falsehood, and the ability to use those principles to deceive and misdirect an opponent), courage, righteousness, wisdom, and benevolence. As Hatsumi-sensei has said, "the sword and the good should go hand in hand."

Cross-Cultural Warrior Virtues

In combining these treatments of the martial virtues, the general approach was to examine the lists produced, and to identify virtues that were common across cultures. If a virtue is endorsed by a wide range of martial traditions, that speaks to its status as a necessary quality of an ideal warrior.

Typical analyses of virtues within the scholarly literature involve attempts to produce a list of "core" virtues, and to demonstrate that other possible virtues may be understood as variations of the core virtue. For example, the virtue of "audacity" may be considered a subtype of the core virtue of "courage." Although audacity is not identical to other forms of courage (such as steadfastness), it may be considered a member of that overall category. Here is a summary of the martial virtues endorsed in the traditions surveyed in this chapter:

Greco-Roman Epic Heroism	Chivalry	Fiore Dei Liberi
Social Status	Prowess	Prudence
Strength	Loyalty	Courage
Beauty	Generosity	Swiftness
Courage	Courtesy	Strength
Skill	Frankness	
Practical Wisdom	Wisdom	
Piety	Justice	
	Courage	
	Temperance	
	Gentleness	
	Ferociousness	
	Strength	
	Charity	

American Heroism	Confucianism	Buddhism	Taoism
Skill	Benevolence	Benevolence	Harmony/Balance
Individualism	Righteousness	Detachment	Spontaneity
Justice	Courteousness		Respect for Life
Practical Wisdom	Wisdom		Non-Action
	Honesty		Moderation
			Filial Piety
			Enlightenment

Yu-Hsia	Shaolin	Hwarang	Bushido
Altruism	Benevolence	Mercy	Justice
Justice	Self-Renunciation	Non-Materialism	Courage
Freedom		Acceptance of Death	Benevolence
Personal Loyalty		Loyalty to the Lord	Politeness
Courage		Filial Piety	Sincerity
Truthfulness		Trustworthiness	Honor
Honor		Never Retreating	Loyalty
Generosity		Justice in Killing	Self-control
			Dignity
			Prudence
			Falling Behind None
			Never Stumbling
			Mercy
			Service
			Self-Sacrifice
			Intelligence
			Humanity
			Pity
			Respect

Ninpo
Devotion to Family and Country
Perseverance
Harmony with Nature
Self-control
Spontaneity
Wisdom
Kyojitsu Tenkan Ho (which I consider to be a form of practical wisdom)
Courage
Righteousness
Benevolence

By combining overlapping virtues and eliminating non-overlapping virtues that appear in only one of the traditions examined, this list can be reduced to the following, which will serve as our categorization of the warrior virtues:

1. Qualities of Effectiveness (strength, skill, speed/swiftness)
2. Courage (ferociousness, audacity, acceptance of death, high spirits)
3. Justice (piety, righteousness, honor, dignity, integrity, sincerity, frankness, honesty, loyalty, devotion, service)

4. Temperance (balance, moderation, non-materialism, self-control)
5. Wisdom (enlightenment, prudence, *kyojitsu tenkan ho*, understanding, love of learning)
6. Benevolence (generosity, liberality, gentleness, charity, compassion, respect for life, altruism, mercy, selflessness, self-sacrifice)

One virtue which appears on more than one of the classic approaches to the warrior virtues, courtesy (or politeness), has been left apart. In the chapter in which I discuss courtesy, I will argue that courtesy is not itself a virtue, but an everyday pattern of behavior in which all the virtues are demonstrated and cultivated.

The first virtuous category listed (the Qualities of Effectiveness) will receive no further attention in this work. I have chosen to leave these qualities unexamined at this time because the focus of this book is on the development of positive personality traits within the context of the martial arts, and also as a recognition of my own personal limitations. I am neither a fitness coach nor a kinesiologist, so I am not qualified to offer advice on the development of physical strength or speed, and far better experts than I have already contributed volumes to the application of physical fitness concepts to the martial arts. Similarly, though I have been a student of the martial arts for quite a few years, by no means would I describe myself as a master. Add to that the questionable value of trying to learn technical skill from a book, the significant differences between the technical aspects of the various martial arts, and the literature written by real masters (again, better experts than I) that already exists, and it becomes clear that including material on the cultivation of technical skill here would be inadvisable. The Qualities of Effectiveness are topics I will leave as a matter between the student and that student's teacher, best handled within their specific art.

In this cross-cultural analysis of warrior virtues, I have explicitly focused my attention on virtue traditions within Western civilization and the Asian traditions of China, Korea, and Japan. Other possibilities exist for consideration of warrior virtues. No consideration, for example, was given in this book to heroic ideals found in Middle Eastern contexts, or to those who draw inspiration from the warrior traditions of the Lakota Sioux in their work on positive character traits.

This level of specificity is employed because this book is directed primarily toward practitioners of the martial arts who wish to delve deeper into the notion of character development and moral growth within their training, and to those outside the martial arts who are giving thought to the value of martial training as a vehicle for improvement in themselves or another. Although exceptions exist (such as the Afro-Brazilian martial art Capoeira), the current majority of English-speaking martial artists operate within an overall Western worldview, and train in an Asian or a Western martial discipline or combative sport. As such, the primary sources of thought on character and ideal warriorhood for this book are Asian ideals derived from Buddhist, Taoist, and Confucian thought, and the Western concepts of moral heroism influenced by classical and medieval scholarship.

Significant variety also exists within cultures. For example, this book does not specifically examine the unique outlook of Aikido founder Morihei Ueshiba. A fully encyclopedic treatment of all possible theories of the warrior virtues across time and culture would be a substantial task in itself, more appropriate for an historian or cultural anthropologist than a psychologist, so what we have covered in this chapter should be considered a representative, rather than exhaustive, presentation of martial traditions. It is my hope that readers who do not "fit the profile" of a Westerner training in a Western or Asian martial art, or who train in an art not specifically mentioned here, will nevertheless find the ideas contained in this book helpful in their specific disciplines.

4

Courage

Cannon to right of them,
Cannon to left of them,
Cannon in front of them
Volleyed and thundered;
Stormed at with shot and shell,
Boldly they rode and well,
Into the jaws of Death,
Into the mouth of Hell
Rode the six hundred.

Alfred, Lord Tennyson
The Charge of the Light Brigade

A truly brave man is ever serene; he is never taken by sur-
prise; nothing ruffles the equanimity of his spirit. In the
heat of battle he remains cool; in the midst of catastrophes
he keeps level his mind. Earthquakes do not shake him, he
laughs at storms.

Inazo Nitobe

The ancient historian Herodotus tells a story containing an act of tremendous courage that has stood as an inspiration for thousands of years. In the fifth century BCE, Darius, King of

Persia, planned to make war on Greece, but died before preparations could be completed, so the task fell to his son Xerxes. Xerxes assembled a massive invasion force and crossed the Hellespont from Asia Minor into Europe. City after city fell before the Persian army. An alliance of Greek city-states, with Athens and Sparta the most prominent, moved to intercept the invading Persians by sea and by land. The only land route large enough for Xerxes' army ran through the narrow pass of Thermopylae, and it was there that one of history's most famous "last stands" took place. Through courage, discipline, and the wise use of geography, a Greek force of about seven thousand held off a Persian force of over two million for three days.

The Greek forces at Thermopylae were led by three hundred Spartans, and it is these Spartans that have received the most attention and admiration. The Spartan attitude is exemplified by the words of Dieneces, who was warned that the Persians were so numerous that, if they all shot their arrows at once, it would block out the sun. "This is pleasant news," replies the Spartan warrior, "for if the Persians hide the sun, we shall have our battle in the shade." Led by King Leonidas, the Spartans turned back one Persian attack after another (to Xerxes' mounting frustration). The Spartans fought until their spears were broken, then they drew their swords. They fought with their swords, their hands, and their teeth, until treachery and overwhelming numbers finally wore them down.[12]

Although Xerxes eventually won the battle, the Persians suffered heavy losses at the hands of the Greeks, and their advance was delayed long enough for a decisive naval battle to occur. Greek warships defeated the Persian navy near the island of Salamis, forcing Xerxes to turn back. Many historians consider the victory at Salamis to be the single most important battle in Western

---

12. This demonstration of bravery directly parallels a passage in *Hagakure*: "If one's sword is broken, he will strike with his hands. If his hands are cut off, he will press the enemy down with his shoulders. If his shoulders are cut away, he will bite through ten or fifteen enemy necks with his teeth. Courage is such a thing."

Civilization. If Xerxes had not been turned back, Greek culture and philosophy likely would not have survived, and our societies would not have been influenced by Greek concepts of justice, democracy, and freedom.

Defining Courage

One of the fundamental truths of the virtues is that they are corrective in nature, "each one standing at a point at which there is some temptation to be resisted or deficiency of maturation to be made good... it is only because fear and the desire for pleasure often operate as temptations that courage and temperance exist as virtues at all." Wisdom is necessary because we are born ignorant and irrational. Benevolence is necessary because we have a tendency toward selfishness. Courage is similarly corrective in nature. We have a natural awareness of our vulnerability to injury and death, and courage counteracts the fear that springs from this awareness. The centrality of fear and vulnerability to the nature of courage forms the basis of the often-heard statement that courage is never to be understood as the absence of fear, but as "doing the right thing in the face of fear."

Varieties of Courage

Most scholars separate courage into two major forms. In the late 19th-century, bushido scholar Inazo Nitobe distinguished between what he calls the "dynamical" and "statical" forms of courage. The dynamical aspect of courage reveals itself in acts of daring, typified by brave acts on the battlefield, while the statical aspect reveals itself in quieter demonstrations of composure and tranquility. This general division of courage into active vs. passive forms is reflected in the philosophy of Joseph Pieper, who distinguishes between courage in "attack" and courage in "endurance," and also in the CSV's distinction between courage as "bravery" and courage as "persistence." That such a diverse set of writers would agree on this two-factor approach to courage argues in favor of the approach's usefulness.

Fiore dei Liberi provides one treatment of the "attack" aspect of courage in his 1410 treatise *Flos Duellatorum*. As described earlier, four virtues (wisdom, courage, speed, and strength) are shown in the "four creatures" illustration in Liberi's treatise. However, one of these virtues is singled out in the prologue of the Pisani-Dossi version of *Flos Duellatorum*, and Liberi calls it "the virtue that makes this art." The virtue that Liberi so elevates is *audatia*, typically translated as "audacity" or "courage." Modern readers may find it odd to use the term "audacity" in this way. Normally, when the words "audacity" or "audacious" are used, they carry the connotation of thoughtlessly trampling standards of polite behavior, and that seems to have questionable applicability to the martial arts. It also contradicts frequent references in other sources to courteous behavior as necessary for a warrior of excellence. However, when properly understood, "audacity" can be seen as a virtue. Audacity as a martial virtue may be defined as a form of courage in which the warrior overcomes fear to act boldly and decisively in the face of danger, without hesitation.

This kind of martial audacity is also seen in Miyamoto Musashi's *Book of Five Rings*, in which Musashi urges aspiring warriors to move from technique to technique without hesitation, and his advice that "as soon as you sense the possibility of an attack, you must react immediately with your own attack to kill the enemy or you will give him the chance to regather himself and come at you again." *Hagakure* contains similar principles, such as Tsunetomo's admonition that "when meeting difficult situations, one should dash forward bravely and with joy," and that "the way of the samurai is one of immediacy, and it is best to dash in headlong."

Audacity in training reflects audacity in combat. Correct training requires taking risks, and audacity is the form of courage that facilitates swift and decisive action in the face of risk. It may be impossible to be fully prepared for the realty of a self-defense situation, but training so as to increase the likelihood of a swift and daring response to an attack could mean the difference between life and death in a real-world conflict.

This might also be seen as one possible reason for sparring as an important component of martial arts training. Although we may engage in debate about exactly how realistic it is to train in the artificial structure of a sparring session, perhaps one of the most important components of this form of training is simply getting used to responding when a fast-moving weapon or bodily structure is coming at you. Virtues are acquired and strengthened through repeated practice, and programs that aim at developing specific virtues often take place in artificial environments (such as classrooms). Putting these principles to work, the argument can be made that being able to respond audaciously when attacked with (for example) a blunt training sword assists in the development of audacity for application in the real world.

Courage has been defined as the overcoming of fear. Persistence, one of the "statical" forms of courage, involves overcoming the fear of failure. This may appear backward to some. Persistence involves not giving up, and one might think that a strong fear of failure would make a person more persistent, not less. But that kind of persistence is a very brittle thing, and can interfere with achieving one's goal.

Failure represents a threat to self-esteem. Nobody wants to see themselves as a failure, and facing the boredom or frustration of a difficult task arouses the temptation to engage in some creative reinterpretations of the task ("It's not really that important," "Nobody could accomplish this," "I have better things to do," "I'm not really feeling like myself today," etc.), that provide an excuse to stop trying. Those who do not try will technically never fail, and thus that person's self-esteem is protected. Courage makes itself known here by facing and defeating that form of ego-defensive fear.

Students of the martial arts should be well acquainted with this form of fear. Training is often repetitive, often effortful, and sometimes painful. The temptation exists to skip training "just this one time," and self-justifying excuses are easily concocted.

The creation of such excuses stems from a fear of seeing oneself as having failed as a martial artist. Two courageous options exist in this situation: One may choose to see through the self-serving justifications and train, even if it is difficult. If one does skip training, then that failure itself provides another opportunity to demonstrate courage. Instead of letting it slide, one may choose to face the fear of failure head-on and refuse to make excuses. Moral courage can involve admitting that the wrong decision was made, and redoubling one's conviction to be faithful to the training next time.

As the ultimate fear is the fear of death, discussions of the ultimate expression of courage involve the ability to face death. Some scholars consider such an ultimate expression to be found by facing death on the battlefield, as did the Spartans at Thermopylae. Others consider a martyr's death to be a higher form of courage, as a fighter at least has a chance (however slim) of victory. A martyr lacks even that consolation, thus requiring greater bravery. Therefore some consider endurance, another "statical" form of courage, to be even more exemplary of courage than a brave attack. Remove any possibility of successful counterattack, and greater amounts of courage are required to face death and pain.

Examples of this kind of courage are easily found. Albanian human rights activist and former political prisoner Fatos Lubonja describes the Albanian communists' treatment of those who were identified as "enemies of the state," offering the choice between confessing to criminal acts (a lie, but one that ensures life), or brutal imprisonment with the possibility of execution. Fannie Lou Hamer, a champion of the Civil Rights Movement, faced tremendous obstacles in her work toward registering Black voters. After being arrested in Winona, Mississippi in 1963, Hamer was subjected to a beating that resulted in permanent damage, damage that eventually contributed to her death. Historian Philip Schaff describes the waves of persecution faced by Christians under various Roman emperors, who employed "all the pains, which iron and steel, fire and sword, rack and cross, wild beasts and beastly men could inflict" to compel an abandonment of their faith. What astounding courage we see in those who are strong enough to remain true in the face of such forces.

Are the courage of the martyr and the courage of the fighter separate strengths, or are they different manifestations of the same strength? Pieper and Nitobe are among those who connect the two strengths. They maintain that courage is courage, so the development and exercise of one form of courage facilitates the other: "The brave man not only knows how to bear inevitable evil with equanimity; he will also not hesitate to 'pounce upon' this evil and to bar its way."

Courage in Interaction with Other Virtues

"What virtue stands alone?" asks Nitobe. As mentioned earlier, scholars speak as one in their insistence that the virtues cannot stand in isolation from each other. Even those who do not try to develop a hierarchical organization around a "master" virtue maintain that good character requires sufficient degrees of all virtues. MacIntyre, whose work is the conceptual foundation for this book, claims that the unity of the virtues is found in the fact that perfection in any one virtue requires perfection in all the virtues. An examination of the functioning of the virtues in the life of a person of good character, then, must include discussions of how virtues interact to provide mutual support and guidance.

Courage is no exception to this principle, requiring other virtues to find its most perfect application. The necessity of justice to a life of courage, for example, is often found in discussions of the virtues. Analyses of courage from sources as varied as Pieper's philosophy, Nitobe's examination of *bushido*, and Goud's use of courage in the counseling process, are insistent that courage is only true when directed toward a just cause. Nitobe, for example, claims that a samurai who lays down his life for an unworthy cause dies "a dogs death," and Gichin Funakoshi, founder of Shotokan karate, follows up his discussion of courage by linking it to the demand that "karate practitioners must stand on the side of justice at all times."

The price of holding to this principle is that we must then apply this high standard to our own actions. Unless our audacity serves justice, we are employing a perversion of courage, and are therefore acting in a way that is not worthy of honor. In the same way that virtue ethics are goal-oriented, directing our development toward an ideal state of being, our actions in specific circumstances must be characterized by a similar focus on our goals. We are motivated by whatever goals we seek in a situation, and we must continually examine our motives so that they serve worthy goals.

In one of his treatises on swordsmanship, 16th-century defense master George Silver admonishes English gentlemen: "Go not into the field with your friend at his entreaty to take his part but first know the manner of the quarrel how justly or unjustly it grew, and do not therein maintain wrong against right, but examine the cause of the controversy, and if there be reason for his rage to lead him to that mortal resolution."

Justice not only directs courage, it also empowers courage. Nakae Toju, a seventeenth-century authority on bushido, demonstrates that samurai who serve a just cause become fearless. As Cleary translates, if the cause is truly worthy, such samurai "are not distracted by desirousness; in establishing justice and reason, acting in a principled way, they are willing to sacrifice their lives for their lords and parents, so they have no fear of death or attachment to life. Because of this, they have nothing to fear between heaven and earth. Facing thousands and myriads of enemies, they are like tigers and wolves facing foxes and badgers, without fear. Having no fear, they are supremely brave."

Another virtue necessary for the demonstration of perfect courage is temperance, the virtue involved in self-control and the moderation of behavior. In his *Nicomachean Ethics*, Aristotle provides us with the "doctrine of the mean," the theory that a virtue is often found in the balance between two vices, with one vice representing a deficiency of the virtue and the other vice representing an excess.

This principle can easily be seen at work in everyday life, with our dietary habits as an example: too much food and we become obese and unable to properly function, too little food and we become malnourished and also unable to properly function. In the chapter on temperance, we will discuss this in more detail.

Temperance is necessary to achieve balance, and courage is considered a classic example of this principle in action. An excess of courage becomes foolhardy recklessness, which can lead to the warrior's death, a lesson learned by Celtic forces at the battle of Cape Telamon in the 3rd century BCE. Celtic warriors were prized for their fierce aggression, often frightening the opposing Roman forces with their daring disregard for their own safety. At Telamon, however, the Romans learned that, by maintaining discipline and holding formation, the Celts' screaming charges could be broken. Counterbalancing our lesson from the battle of Thermopylae, the battle of Cape Telamon is seen by some as a victory of disciplined courage over intemperate recklessness.

While an excess of courage is recklessness, a deficiency of courage is cowardice. Although this punishment is very rare, cowardice in battle does still carry the possibility of the death penalty according to Article 99 of the United States' Uniform Code of Military Justice,[13] and many members of the armed forces consider desertion to be one of the most reprehensible actions possible.

---

13. "Any member of the armed forces who before or in the presence of the enemy (1) runs away; (2) shamefully abandons, surrenders, or delivers up any command, unit, place, or military property which it is his duty to defend; (3) through disobedience, neglect, or intentional misconduct endangers the safety of any such command, unit, place, or military property; (4) casts away his arms or ammunition; (5) is guilty of cowardly conduct; (6) quits his place of duty to plunder or pillage; (7) causes false alarms in any command, unit, or place under control of the armed forces; (8) willfully fails to do his utmost to encounter, engage, capture, or destroy any enemy troops, combatants, vessels, aircraft, or any other thing, which it is his duty so to encounter, engage, capture, or destroy; or (9) does not afford all practicable relief and assistance to any troops, combatants, vessels, or aircraft of the armed forces belonging to the United States or their allies when engaged in battle; shall be punished by death or such other punishment as a court-martial may direct."

Temperance assists in striking the appropriate balance between recklessness and cowardice, where true courage exists.

In *The Republic*, Plato gives thought to the qualities of character of society's guardians. He was troubled by the possibility that, left unguided, the aggressiveness of Greek warriors would lead them to turn on each other, and to destroy the very society that they were intended to protect. Plato's prescription to correct for this possibility was that aggressive "high spirits" must be guided by the wisdom to discern between appropriate and inappropriate targets for their ferocity. While guiding courage with justice directs one's actions toward worthy goals, wisdom enables one to know which goals are worthy. When guided by wisdom, daring acts harm only those who must be harmed, and protect those who must be protected. This makes wisdom a virtue that must also be cultivated in any person who wishes to become more courageous.

Psychologist Blaine Fowers describes practical wisdom in terms of "moral perception." Wisdom allows the individual to quickly and accurately "size up" a situation, seeing what the important elements of that situation are, what goal is to be pursued, and the best way to pursue that goal. Fowers' claim that "moral perception will often result in a clear and immediate response and the appropriate course of action will be immediately apparent" shows that wisdom is a practical as well as admirable partner with courage.

Audacity, an aspect of courage, involves taking swift and decisive action in the face of danger. Cultivating wisdom, which accelerates one's ability to quickly perceive the correct course of action in a given situation, would therefore make one's audacious actions even more swift and decisive.

Cultivating Courage in Yourself

Describe courage, not as the absence of fear, but as the ability to accomplish necessary tasks in the presence of fear, and fear becomes an opponent to be faced and defeated rather than denied. Social psychologist John Dollard conducted a study of 300 combat veterans, examining variables that enabled them to defeat fear in battle. Among the factors that he found to have an impact were (1) early identification of fear, (2) fear suppression, (3) distraction, (4) humanization of the enemy, and (5) identification with a cause.

(1) Early identification of fear: Dollard recommends that soldiers prepare themselves to counteract fear well ahead of time, noting that "the soldier who knows he will be afraid and tries to get ready for it makes a better soldier." Numerous psychological studies have been conducted which demonstrate that mentally rehearsing a task ahead of time increases the ease and effectiveness of performing the behavior. The ability to carry out a task depends on how strongly the procedure is represented in memory, and mentally preparing for a task strengthens that representation. Mentally rehearsing fear-countering tasks improves one's ability to engage in those tasks. Knowing that we will face a particular danger allows for the opportunity to think about how we will react in that situation. This increases the ease with which we will carry out the desired behavior despite the fear. Martial artists can put this principle to work by spending time imagining attacks as they practice, by posing hypothetical self-defense scenarios to themselves, and visualizing themselves remaining calm during fights.

(2) Suppression of fear: Dollard's description of fear "suppression" in the battlefield does not involve denying that fear exists, but instead involves "pretending" that we are calm rather than afraid. One key insight into human nature that we can gather from the field of psychology is that our thoughts, emotions, and behaviors are locked together in a relationship of mutual influence. What happens to one affects the others. Numerous studies support the idea that carrying out the kinds of behaviors that are associated with a particular emotion or idea will increase the likelihood of actually experiencing the emotion or believing the idea, so that what a person thinks or feels is influenced by what that person is doing. One team of researchers, for example, manipu-

lated research participants (by asking them to hold a pen in their teeth) into holding their faces in a way that simulated a smile. These participants experienced more intense humorous reactions to cartoons. Emotions can be altered by altering behaviors. So even if you do not feel brave at the moment... fake it. Forcing calm behavior in the face of danger can result in genuine calmness, enhancing your ability to do what is necessary in the face of danger.

(3) Distraction: Distraction functions similarly to fear suppression. By forcing your attention to some detail unrelated to the danger (Dollard's examples include completing mundane tasks like the inspection of gear, concentrating on "setting a good example" for one's companions, and thinking of a good joke to break the tension), calmness is enhanced and it becomes easier to "fake" courage. Empirical research into such activities have supported Dollard's claim that they may serve as useful techniques for combating fear.

(4) Humanization of the enemy: Seeing your opponent as human involves the realization that your opponent is experiencing the same range of emotions as yourself, especially fear. The tactic of attempting to convince the enemy that you are more (or less) than human has a long and consistent tradition in warfare, with examples including Norse berserkers, the legends linking ninja to the mysterious *tengu* (mountain goblins), and the frenzied displays of the ancient Celts. See through these facades, and your opponent loses considerable power. In the ring, an opponent may look superhuman, but we both know that to be a false front (You may find it helpful to take just a moment to imagine your opponent doing something embarrassingly human.).

(5) Identification with a cause: Dollard says that "Fear is not controlled by mental magic. It is controlled by making other forces stronger than it." Among the forces that counteract fear in battle, one of the most powerful identified in Dollard's research was identification with a cause. Believing in the rightness of the war being fought, and the foundational ideas of one's country, strongly

counteracted fear in battle. This principle has been convincingly demonstrated by the psychological research conducted using terror management theory. This theory examines the role of people's beliefs and values in connection to death-related fear. Humans are described by terror management theorists as unique among animals in our ability to think about the future. This advanced cognitive ability brings with it an awareness of inevitable mortality, and anxiety over the idea of our eventual death. This death-related fear is managed by holding to a shared cultural worldview, which provides a description of meaning in life, standards of value, and the promise of some form of victory over death. Examples of the types of values, and forms of immortality, offered by such a worldview include the valuing of family, with the survival of your offspring serving as a vicarious immortality; the production of works of art, with symbolic immortality found in the notion that something of yourself will continue to exist and influence people after your own death; and adherence to religious beliefs, with a literal immortality promised in the afterlife. The research findings of both terror management theorists and Dollard point to the ability of strong beliefs to overpower our natural fear of death, to the point where people are able to deliberately lay down their lives if necessary. Fear can be defeated by believing in something greater than oneself, something worth living for, something worth dying for.

The examples given above are methods of conquering fear in specific situations. Regarding the cultivation of bravery as an overall personality trait, the psychological research literature is of little help, as almost no empirical research has been done on bravery, and the CSV's survey of the applied scholarly literature reveals no proven methods for fostering courage as a trait. Instead, the CSV's authors suggest possible methods for the development of bravery based on research into related variables.

The study of courageous role models increases the likelihood of performing brave acts oneself. In an early therapeutic application of social learning theory, children who had previously experienced fear of dogs watched a non-phobic child having fun playing with a cocker spaniel. After several sessions observing this model, the dog-phobic children demonstrated a decrease in their fear, and an increased willingness to approach and play with the dog. Applying these principles to our topic, watching other people doing things that we are afraid to do will increase our ability to overcome that fear. Social learning researchers have also found that moral excellence can be learned through the observation of parents, peers, and television/movie characters both real and fictional.

Observational learning can also take place through stories. The emotional state of identifying with the main character increases the likelihood that readers will incorporate the loves, hates, values, and characteristics of that character, making the reading of books a powerful tool in the cultivation of the virtues. Applied to courage, the practice of reading stories of courageous heroes assists in the development of courage in the reader.

Inazo Nitobe discusses the role that courage-centered stories played in the cultivation of bravery in young members of samurai families. From a very young age, such children were encouraged to be brave in the face of adversity, and told frequent stories of courageous warriors.

As with the other virtues, courage is acquired through habitual action. This presents a small problem for the cultivation of courage, as our prototypical image of a courageous action requires a life-threatening situation, and these are (in most people's lives) very infrequent. More everyday acts of courage, however, are in greater supply, and can be employed toward the cultivation of this virtue. At an emotional level, for example, several psychologists connect courage with the emotional vulnerability of a committed marriage. As an intimate relationship contains the potential for tremendous pain, courage is required to maintain a well-functioning marriage, and thus daily acts of relational vulnerability are acts of everyday bravery.

Nitobe, focusing on the "spiritual aspect of valour," makes the claim that courage is demonstrated as composure in everyday situations ("Tranquility is courage in repose"). Focusing on developing calmness in the face of the thousand setbacks and minor threats faced in a typical day can assist with the development of a courage that might only find full expression in a very few life-or-death circumstances. By doing this, not only are we cultivating a warrior's way of life, we are freeing ourselves from the stress of fearful reactions to normal events such as a careless driver who cuts in front of you on the highway, expressing an opinion that may meet with disapproval from one's friends, facing the possibility of rejection by a potential romantic partner, or the embarrassment of asking a "stupid question" in a classroom. By developing the "statical" forms of bravery, we are also developing the "dynamical" forms.

I have found Chögyam Trungpa's description of a warrior's confident walk to be a useful visualization for demonstrating a courageous approach to everyday life: "The tiger walks slowly through the jungle, with mindfulness. But... he is relaxed. From the tip of his nose to the tip of his tail, there are no problems. His movements are like waves; he swims through the jungle. So his watchfulness is accompanied by relaxation and confidence. This is the analogy for the warrior's confidence."

Counseling psychologist Nelson Goud suggests the taking of risks and expansion of one's "comfort zone" as methods for the cultivation of courage. Such activities (Goud lists rock climbing, willingness to speak up for what is right, and martial arts training among the examples) involve taking a desired action in the face of danger, making them suitable activities for the cultivation of courage.

Previously, bravery was discussed using the cognitive-behavioral perspective of social learning theory. Now we will turn our attention to the technique of systematic desensitization, which is derived from Pavlovian conditioning principles. Pavlovian conditioning focuses on changing the way that people respond to events in the environment, and systematic desensitization program aims at producing a calm response. This kind of program is often used to help people who have a phobia in their attempts to reduce their fear of some object. The person is taught various calming techniques (muscle relaxation practices, breathing exercises, visualization, etc), and these methods are employed while the client is systematically exposed to increasingly intense levels of exposure to whatever the object is that they are afraid of.

For example, a client with a snake phobia might first engage in the calming techniques while listening to someone talk about snakes. Once the client is able to listen to someone talk about snakes while remaining calm, the therapy might progress to looking at pictures of snakes, then to handling a rubber toy snake, then to being in a room with a live snake in a cage, and so on. Eventually, the client is able to pick up and handle a live snake while remaining in a calm state. This method of counteracting chronic fears has enjoyed widespread success, and has been applied to anxieties ranging from phobias and nightmares to test anxiety and fear of public speaking.

Most systematic desensitization programs contain some form of mental imagery. In some cases, the early levels of exposure to the feared object involve thinking about it, reading about it, or talking about it. This is done so that the client can begin with a very mild level exposure. In other cases, the feared stimulus may be something that cannot easily be physically encountered as a part of the therapeutic process (such as a fear of flying, in which it would be tremendously difficult to set up a program involving a gradually-increasing exposure to airline travel). The mental components of systematic desensitization may also be used when the phobia involves an abstract concept (One team of psychologists report the use of these kinds of treatments in helping a person who had an exaggerated fear of communism), including abstract concepts such as the inescapable reality of death.

Hagakure contains a passage in which a mental practice is described which may also be understood in terms of behavioral psychology, and may be of some use in cultivating calmness in the face of danger:

> Meditation on inevitable death should be performed daily. Every day when one's body and mind are at peace, one should meditate upon being ripped apart by arrows, rifles, spears and swords, being carried away by surging waves, being thrown into the midst of a great fire, being struck by lightning, being shaken to death by a great earthquake, falling from thousand-foot cliffs, dying of disease or committing seppuku at the death of one's master. And every day without fail one should consider himself as dead.

In every respect, from relaxation to the imaginary exposure to relevant stimuli, this meditative technique mirrors the mental imagery component of systematic desensitization. Distressing thoughts are paired with a calm response, decreasing (perhaps not completely eliminating, but decreasing) the likelihood that the same objects in the real world will produce a fearful response.

Dave Lowry recounts the story of a samurai who approached a swordmaster for instruction. When the two faced each other to begin training, the master accused the student of being a master himself, and asked why he had lied about being a mere novice. The student expressed perplexity, as he was no swordmaster. Upon further questioning, the student explained: "Early on, when I showed no aptitude for fencing or any other of the *bujutsu* (warrior arts), I concluded that as a *bushi* (warrior) I would probably die in battle very quickly. Therefore, I spent all of my time contemplating my own death. I kept it in my thoughts constantly, no matter what I was doing. Over the years, it was an ever-present companion, until I realized that I was no longer afraid to die. I have passed beyond any concern about it at all." Upon hearing this, the swordmaster presented the student with a certificate of mastery, claiming that he had already attained the highest possible level of martial accomplishment.

Short of deliberately (foolishly) exposing oneself to life-threatening events, mental disciplines such as this might be as close as is reasonably possible for a deliberate everyday bravery-enhancing exercise involving the topic of death.

Cultivating Courage in Others

Similar to their review of the research on the cultivation of bravery within oneself, the authors of CSV find that little work has been done on directly fostering bravery in others, so we are again required to adapt principles from related lines of research. Those (instructors, parents, teachers, leaders, etc) who wish to assist others in their growth toward higher levels of bravery may find some help in the research on "transformational leadership." Transformational leadership is a way of leading others, in which followers are inspired rather than bullied or manipulated. There are four major components of this style of leadership, components that reflect much of what has already been covered in terms of cultivating courage within oneself.

(1) Idealized influence: Management expert Niro Sivanathan and his colleagues state that transformational leaders inspire by doing "what is right, rather than what is expedient, simple, or cost-effective." We have covered some ways in which people can learn courage by adopting courageous role models. Leaders can inspire courage in others by demonstrating courage themselves, thus becoming someone's role model.

(2) Inspirational motivation: By focusing students' attention toward what can be accomplished rather than what obstacles exist, by telling stories of achievement, and by structuring activities in such a way that goals become attainable and rewarded, principles such as learned industriousness (which we discuss below) and mental rehearsal can be employed toward the cultivation of courage in others.

(3) Intellectual stimulation: Transformational leaders do not attempt to present themselves as having all the answers, but rather encourage followers to seek out answers and to question assumptions. One suggestion for teachers of the martial arts is to avoid presenting oneself as The Master, Keeper of All Martial Truth. No matter the length of our training or the extent of our experience, we remain students. Admitting this allows students

to see being like the instructor as an attainable goal (in his chapter on role models, Michael Cohn focuses on the idea that, for a model to be effective at inspiring excellence, the goal of being like the model must be attainable), and prevents the disillusionment that can come when the student realizes the imperfection of the role model.

(4) Individualized consideration: By establishing and maintaining good personal relationships with each individual subordinate, a leader provides an environment in which personal feelings and aspiration can freely be expressed. This can facilitate the relational bravery that, as previously discussed, can contribute to other forms of bravery.

Earlier in this chapter, we worked with the idea that we can connect persistence, the tendency not to give up when situations become difficult, to the courageous overcoming of the fear of failure. This makes persistence one of the "statical" forms of courage, in which one faces the possibility of a humiliating failure, and continues to push toward the goal. Unlike the research into bravery, the development of persistence has been empirically examined. Reviewing numerous studies on the topic, Robert Eisenberger found that accomplishing tasks that require persistence can lead to an overall increase in persistence. Whether the exercise involves exerting physical or mental effort, or enduring discomfort in the process of reaching a goal, humans can demonstrate what Eisenberger called "learned industriousness." By presenting people with difficult, but attainable, goals, and then rewarding them for success, they can be taught to believe in their ability to overcome obstacles through persistent effort.

This kind of persistence training is easily applicable to the martial arts. Martial training presents students with numerous physical and mental challenges. Instructors may find that their curriculum is already set up in such a way that students are given goals that require effort, but are within their power, and carry some reward. For example, many arts have a fairly elaborate system of belt ranks, offering the possibility of frequent testing and advancement. If such a system is handled improperly, it becomes a transparent ploy to soak students for more money through repeated testing fees and the sale of new belts. If handled properly, though, such a system could be an opportunity to develop persistence by showing students that they can succeed in the face of obstacles. This claim is likely to be a controversial one, as the majority opinion in the martial arts community is that rapid advancement through ever-proliferating belts is a classic strategy of the "McDojo," combining low quality of training with a high degree of exploitative profit-mongering. I entirely understand this objection and partially share it ("Hot pink" belts? Camouflage-colored belts? And you expect me to take your dojo seriously?). But *if done properly*, there may be something to salvage from this system. Part of the development of the virtues includes the idea that, as one becomes stronger, one is going to be capable of greater virtuous acts. But at early levels, the student might only be capable of minor acts of virtue. So there may be some wisdom in letting the lowest-level students progress rapidly through the first few levels, with the requirements in both time and skill increasing the further along one goes (some arts already use this approach).

The principles previously covered may be employed toward the development of courage in other people in other ways, as well. Students may be encouraged to engage in the individual practices previously described. Praising students for persistent or daring acts can have a powerful effect, as can encouraging and rewarding calmness in the face of adversity.

Conclusion

Courage, in its diverse forms, is a great asset to one who wishes to engage in martial training. By performing the necessary actions in the face of fear and pain in training, it becomes more likely that the student will correctly perform these behaviors in actual defensive situations. Courage is also an asset to one who wishes to develop their overall character. While others virtues guide and complement courage, it is courage that provides the strength necessary to carry out admirable acts in the face of opposition.

5

Justice

This sword I have been polishing for ten years;
Its frosty edge has never been put to the test.
Now that I've shown it to you, pray tell me:
Is there anyone suffering from injustice?

Chia Tao

Fiat justitia et ruant coeli.
Let justice be done, though the heavens fall.

William Watson

A classic story of loyalty in action is the tale of the 47 ronin. In 1701, Kira Yoshinaka, an official in the court of Shogun Tokugawa Tsunayoshi in Japan, repeatedly insulted Naganori Asano, a powerful lord. Although Asano did his best to overlook the ongoing provocation, he eventually lost his temper and attacked Kira. Because this took place in Edo castle, where drawing a weapon was forbidden, this offense was punishable by death. Asano was required to commit *seppuku* (ritual suicide), his family was ruined, and his samurai were reduced to the status of *ronin* (masterless samurai).

Forty-seven of these ronin made a secret pledge to avenge their master, and embarked on an elaborate plan. They went their separate ways, taking whatever jobs they could find, marginalized by Japanese society. Convinced that the ronin posed no threat, Kira eventually relaxed his guard. A year after his original offense, the ronin slowly infiltrated the city in which Kira lived, assembled weapons and armor, and assaulted his mansion on December 14th, 1702. Kira was killed, and the ronin accepted the death sentence for murder (the Shogun, unsure how to handle warriors who showed great loyalty but broke the law, compromised by giving them an honorable death by seppuku).

These ronin were willing to go through humiliation and death to avenge their lord. They were buried with their master at Sengaku-ji temple, and to this day many visitors burn incense and pay their respects at the graves. This act of loyalty is considered one of Japan's great culture-forming historical events, the ronin are referred to as *gishi* (righteous samurai), and their story has inspired numerous plays, novels, movies, and works of art.

Defining Justice

Irish political philosopher Allyn Fives defines the virtue of justice as "the disposition to govern one's conduct according to rules of justice." But what are the rules of justice? Attempts to define the fundamental nature of justice are as old as philosophy itself, and no consensus has ever been reached among scholars.

In one of his examinations of justice, MacIntyre describes multiple conflicting definitions that have arisen across the centuries, a wide range of ideas from such a diverse group as Isocrates (a contemporary of Plato), Augustine, and the mutually-contradictory claims of various Enlightenment thinkers (such as Rousseau, Bentham, Kant, the authors of the *Encyclopédie*, and the philosophers of Scottish "common sense realism"). Despite many attempts to search for common ground, MacIntyre concludes that "modern academic philosophy turns out by and large to provide means for a more accurate and informed definition of disagreement rather than for progress toward its resolution."

Instead of attempting to put forward a single approach to the virtue of justice, our focus will be on conducting a very brief sketch of a few different applicable definitions of justice, and examining how these justices may be applied in the life of the martial artist.

Plato's masterwork *The Republic*, written in the 4th century BC, centers around the question "What is justice?" Attempting to answer that question leads the characters in the book to consider issues as far-reaching as war, psychology, anthropology, morality, metaphysics, utopian politics, education, and the afterlife. Platonic thought on justice was based on the belief that "the universe is the manifestation of a single pervading law, and that human life is good so far as it obeys that law." Justice is therefore defined as a life lived in harmony with the moral structure of the universe, a notion that is reminiscent of Taoist thought on the nature of right behavior. This principle explains the broad scope of Plato's philosophical examination. If justice is a truly universal principle, then it is relevant to all aspects of existence, from the completion of a business deal, to the policy of the schools, to the basic structure of society, to the relationship between human and heaven, to the functions of one's own thoughts and emotions.

To be a just person within this definition is to be someone whose life "fits" in the order of the universe. The elements of one's mind (desires, intellect, etc) and of one's life (work, family, friendships, etc.) each carry out their proper function in the proper way to the proper degree. When interacting with other people, those people are treated in a manner that fits their place in the universe. That is a just act. To call an act unjust is, in the words of political philosopher Geoffrey Cupit, to say that it is "an unfitting act; it is an act which fails to accord with the status of the person treated."

Describing what treatment fits a person's status introduces the concept of *just desert* into matters of justice. If a person deserves a reward, justice is ensuring that the person gets that reward; if a person deserves punishment, justice is ensuring that the person is punished (the treatment fits their status). Philosopher James

Sterba claims that all major approaches to the concept of justice within current debate still agree that justice consists of giving people what they deserve. The disagreements center around exactly what people deserve, and how to give it to them.

Applications of this definition of justice can be found in many areas of life. Within the field of education, some teachers complain that they sometimes face pressure from parents, students, and administrators to distribute grades in a manner that does not fit a student's performance. At the university level, some professors have noticed a growing sense of entitlement among students, grounded in a consumer-oriented mindset. Some students believe that they should pass a course because they paid for it, not because their performance merits a good grade. As a professor, if I bowed to this pressure, I would be committing an injustice, treating students in a manner that does not fit their status.

This same consumer-oriented injustice can also be seen in the less-reputable martial arts schools. Instructors perpetrate a tremendous injustice if they establish "black belt contract" systems that *guarantee* promotion to black belt status if a certain amount of money is paid.

Considerations of justice also may be applied to verbal behavior such as compliments or insults. To praise someone too highly is an unjust act (and may result in acquiring a reputation as an insincere flatterer), because the person has done little or nothing to deserve the praise. Similarly, an insult is an unjust act, because it involves treating the person as if they are lower in status than they truly are.

Verbal justice therefore consists of speaking about someone exactly as they deserve, neither better nor worse. Verbal injustice within the martial arts may involve such behaviors as badmouthing a rival school in order to draw more students to one's own dojo, or speaking disrespectfully about an opponent's skill. Speaking too highly of someone's skill is also an injustice, often seen in the immature "my sensei can beat up your sensei" arguments one encounters in internet discussion boards.

As students and practitioners of the martial arts, the definition of justice as getting one's just desert plays a tremendous role in our conduct. We are engaged in the study of violent behavior, and the greater our skill, the greater the potential for harm. It is vital that we deal with people in a manner that fits what they deserve. Consider, for example, the various degrees of just desert that we may encounter in a fight. A drunken idiot who throws a couple of sloppy half-hearted punches while you escort him to his taxi does not deserve the same level of response as an armed rapist leaping from his place of concealment along a jogging path. As fans of the Spider-Man comics can tell you, power and responsibility go hand in hand. Martial training makes us powerful, and that increases our responsibility to act justly, causing no undue harm.

While classical approaches to justice focus on *relative* status and just desert (treating people differently because of the different things we deserve), theories of right action that are influenced by the thought of Immanuel Kant focus more on matters of humans' *universal* status as humans (treating people the same based on what we all share). Kant's approach to moral philosophy centered on the identification of universal laws of behavior, and demands the treatment of all people in accordance with those laws. The universal status of people is different from the status of objects. We use objects to accomplish our goals; they are means to an end. People are not objects; they possess worth and dignity in themselves. We must treat them accordingly.

Former US Marine Captain (and renowned martial artist) Jack Hoban claims that the foundation of ethical warriorship is to treat all human life as equally valuable, even the lives of our enemies. Unethical warriorship involves treating the lives of those who oppose you as having less value, making it "okay" to sacrifice them to achieve your goals (terrorists targeting crowds of civilians are an excellent example of this). In Kantian terms, we are always to treat people as "ends in themselves," never as only means.

Disreputable "McDojos" can again serve as an example of this principle in action. Whatever the specific offense may be (long-term contracts without the option to withdraw, requiring students to only use overpriced gear or uniforms purchased from the instructor, adding new ranks for the purposes of collecting more testing fees), exploiting students' inexperience so that the instructor can squeeze as much money as possible out of them is an injustice. It treats students as nothing more than means to a financial end.

The worth and dignity of people must be recognized and respected as we interact with them. Philosopher Hardy Jones argued that this is to be accomplished in two ways. First, we are to avoid using people to achieve goals to which they cannot rationally consent. Theft is an immoral action because nobody can rationally decide that they want to be robbed. Slavery is an immoral social system because no rational person can desire to be a slave. A dojo with an exploitative pricing scheme is immoral because nobody can rationally desire to be exploited. Second, Jones argues that we treat people with the respect to which they are due by actively placing a high priority on their welfare, seeking to advance their happiness. People must be treated with benevolence, no matter what your feelings toward them might be.

Theologian Harry Emerson Fosdick connected the moral notions found in this definition of justice to the Golden Rule: Do to others as you would have them do to you. He claims that "simple justice involves the treatment of another's personality as, equally with one's own, an object of respect and consideration. A just man, therefore, must refuse to claim for himself what he is unwilling to grant to others."[14] This task requires a certain degree of imagination, as we must picture ourselves in the other person's place, and attempt to understand how we would wish to be treated if we were in the other person's place. Fosdick explains, "When a man does as he would be done by, he judges fairly, speaks kindly, refuses to exploit personality for private gain, protects the weak,

---

14. Harry Emerson Fosdick, *The Meaning of Service* (New York: Association Press, 1927), 91. (Note: When Fosdick uses the term "personality," he is referring to someone's status as a person.)

rescues the fallen, and treats even his enemies as though they might some day become his friends."

To continue with our example of the exploitative dojo, imagine that you are a student (for those of you who in fact are students, this will be easy). Would you desire to pay exorbitant amounts of money for low-quality instruction?

While the first definition of justice that we've covered (Plato's) emphasizes the need to treat people differently based on what they deserve, this second definition (Kant's) emphasizes the need to treat people equally, based on our shared nature. These two principles do not necessarily exist in conflict, as it might appear. Treating others based on what they deserve involves applying certain principles of justice. Equality involves the application of those principles in an impartial manner, not biasing your judgment. We all have a tendency to "spin" our decision-making processes based on our own benefit, and for the benefit of "our people" at the expense of outsiders. Committing to treat people with equality requires that we act in opposition to that tendency. If principles of just desert are applied equally, outcomes will not always be the same, because people's behavior will not always be the same, but the "criterion of treatment" will be equal.

As we have seen, applying Kant's notion of justice to martial arts instructors means not treating students as nothing more than means to an end. What does this definition of justice mean to martial arts students? In training, treating other students as means to an end may involve seeing them as sources of entertainment or as nothing more than vehicles for their own advancement. Sparring becomes an opportunity to bully weaker fighters. When practicing techniques, insufficient attention is given to helping one's fellow students learn, or insufficient attention is given to their safety.

Treating your fellow students as ends in themselves means giving them all the consideration and respect that you would wish for from them. You should place as much effort toward their advancement as toward your own. Be attentive to their safety, and considerate in the infliction of pain. Do not humiliate them when they are defeated, and accept defeats without bitterness. Instructors should be treated with the same degree of respect that you would desire if you were in their place.

This approach to justice becomes more difficult in a real-world self-defense situation. Is it possible to show respect and consideration for an attacker? We should imagine ourselves in the attacker's place; but can we? I don't know if I can. This is a hard principle, not easily applied. Fosdick's statement about treating our enemies as if they might one day become our friends requires that we only inflict the amount of damage necessary in a situation.

This approach to justice also demands that physical confrontation be our last resort. Seeing our opponents as people who possess dignity and value equal to our own brings with it an extreme reluctance to destroy that which has such incalculable worth. Putting this principle to work, fights must be entered into unwillingly, reluctantly, and with a profound sense of regret. Martial artist (and RAND Corporation foreign policy expert) Forrest Morgan, also working from the belief that today's enemy should be treated as if he may be tomorrow's ally, recommends that confrontations be resolved in such a way that the opponent does not "lose face" (suffer a blow to their pride). Warriors often suffer from a tendency toward excess of ego, and will fight to avoid loss of face. Conflicts may be de-escalated if small concessions are made that allow one's opponent to back off without appearing weak or fearful.

Political philosopher John Rawls is considered by many to be the most influential twentieth-century thinker on the topic of justice. His primary book, *A Theory of Justice*, approaches justice from a very different perspective than our previous two viewpoints. Rawls' ideas reflect a "social contract" approach to justice. This involves the idea that people enter into agreements with each other, and that justice consists of fulfilling those agreements. In a contract, each side has its rights and its obligations.

Most examples of social contract theory in action involve how we see the relationship between the government and the citizens of a country. The government's side of the contract is to defend the citizens, provide certain vital services that the citizens cannot provide alone, and violate people's rights only when it is absolutely necessary for society to function (punishing people who commit fraud or perjury might technically be thought of as violations of the right to free speech, but they are necessary and reasonable violations).

Citizens, in turn, are obligated to maintain their side of the contract: to obey the laws, to accept the necessary and reasonable restrictions to their rights out of a sense of enlightened self-interest, and to support the government through such activities as military service, paying taxes, and holding public office. If either side breaks the contract, they face consequences. A citizen who breaks the law faces punishment, and a government that oppresses rather than defends the people may, as the key players in the American Revolution argued, be justly overthrown and replaced (America's Declaration of Independence is directly based on social contract theory, and I have found it to be one of the most clear and eloquent expressions of these principles available).

Scholarly work within this tradition has primarily focused on the society-level questions of justice; the most fair system for distributing economic resources, the correct treatment of criminals, and so on. Less has been said about this approach to justice in individual behavior, which is a more important issue for our exploration of justice as a personal virtue.

Rawls admits that the focus of his books and his theory is primarily on matters of social justice rather than individual justice, but he does give personal behavior some consideration in *A Theory of Justice*. Rawls' application of justice to individual behavior involves the idea that we are in contract with each one another, just as much as citizens are with the government. As partners in the social contract, we are to refrain from harming each other, help each other when in jeopardy, and "play by the rules" of our respective social roles (with the understanding that, if the others are good partners, they will do their share as well. They will refrain from harming us, will help us when we need it, and will themselves play by the rules).

Such an approach to the just martial artist might center on the warrior's role in society. From Rawls' viewpoint, when one agrees to take on a social role (spouse, business partner, judge, etc), one is obligated to act in a way that fits with the rules of that position. A spouse is obligated to remain faithful, a business partner is forbidden to embezzle, a judge must rule with impartiality, and so on. A warrior's duty is to protect. By agreeing to enter into martial training, the student is entering into a contract that obligates that person to act as a protector of those who require his or her services. Even if the martial artist does not belong to a profession that involves formally working as a protector (such as the military or law enforcement), status as an "amateur warrior" still carries with it the duty to act as a protector whenever able. Dr. Robert Humphrey's "Warrior Creed" includes the statement "Wherever I walk, everyone is a little bit safer because I am there."

Another contractual element to the martial arts involves the training itself. We take on obligations to our fellow students when we enter into training. There are, for example, the obligations that come with the drilling of techniques. The standard approach in training involves one partner beginning with an attack, and the other partner responds with the technique being practiced. In the Japanese arts, the term *uke* is used to describe one who plays the role of attacker, while *tori* is used to describe one who responds with the technique. When training in this capacity, the uke is obligated to begin with an attack that is committed and energetic, but properly controlled, and without genuine intent to injure; and the severity of the attack is to be moderated to match the skill level of the tori. The tori is obligated to execute the appropriate techniques with a similar balance of intensity and gentleness.

Obligations also characterize the teacher-student contract. Martial arts instructors are obligated to provide quality instruction, and to avoid irresponsible practices that violate this obligation, such as unrealistic claims (an example would be the "I Will

Make You an Unstoppable Death Machine" advertisements seen in some martial arts magazines), excessively dangerous training techniques, or exploitive pricing schemes. Students also have obligations toward their instructors. Examples include obedience to reasonable orders, faithful attendance, and adherence to whatever reasonable payment plan has been agreed upon.

Varieties of Justice

Justice to the Self: Honor and Integrity

So far, the examples of justice provided have exclusively involved interpersonal behavior. This is understandable, as discussions of justice most often are social and political in nature, leading the authors of the CSV to characterize justice-related character strengths as "relevant to the optimal interaction between the individual and the group or the community." But virtue theorists have also connected notions of justice to the self. Although the question of justice typically involves the ways to treat others justly, it is also possible to discuss ways to treat yourself justly. It is in this context that I will discuss such concepts as honor and integrity.

Honor is justice turned inward. It is my belief that the role of honor in the warrior's life may be best understood as the treatment of oneself in accordance with the principles of just desert, dignity, and social role. Honor is a troublesome concept, both inherently social and transcending society. To say that something is honored requires a group to place a high value on that thing (making "honor" the same as "reputation"), but many of the greatest examples of honorable behavior are found in those who have defied popular opinion, and placed their personal moral convictions above the dictates of the group. Forrest Morgan claims that honor is entirely about fulfilling obligations, and has nothing to do with reputation, while historian Eugen Weber makes the opposing claim that honor is and always has been entirely about reputation. In his examination of how concepts of honor influenced the American South, Bertram Wyatt-Brown says that throughout history our ideas about honor have always had to deal with this tension between its personal and social natures.

An early example of this tension is the Roman philosopher Cicero, and his writings on honor in *De Officiis* (44 BCE). Cicero makes the claim that a good man is someone whose actions would be honored by other good men. There can, of course, be many reasons why one specific action does not actually receive honor in the real world. There may be no witnesses to the action, or the action may have been observed by people who are less than honorable, or the action may have been misunderstood. But "even if it is not accorded acclaim, it is still honorable" (*De Officiis*, I:14).

While it may be possible to theoretically disentangle honor from public reputation, issues of honor have been linked to issues of prestige throughout history. The *Illiad* begins with a dispute between Achilles and Agamemnon over a matter of honor involving who gets a better share of the spoils of war. Inazo Nitobe tells of the samurai's tendency toward hypersensitivity regarding insults and public disgrace. Maurice Keen's analysis of chivalry involves an examination of the aristocratic pride and thirst for glory that characterized the knightly class.

Alexandre Dumas' *The Three Musketeers* paints a picture of seventeenth-century French swordsmen who dueled at every opportunity over the smallest perceived slights to their honor, and he said of his novel's young hero that "d'Artagnan considered every smile an insult, and even a look as a provocation. Therefore, his fist was doubled from Tarbes to Meung; and, from one cause or another, his hand was on the pommel of his sword ten times a day." Kenneth Greenberg describes the tendency of gentlemen in the American pre-Civil-War South to enter into duels over insults ranging from the tweaking of a nose, to failure to show the proper respect during an argument over a trifling issue, to comments regarding body odor: "When the man of honor is told that he smells, he does not take a bath—he draws his pistol."

While instances such as these may be examples of excessive sensitivity, they are at least comprehensible if honor is thought of as the application of justice to oneself. Eighteenth-century philosopher/satirist Bernard Mandeville connected the idea of honor to humanity's natural tendency toward self-esteem, and a refusal to be under-valued by anyone. Line up this concept with Cupit's definition of injustice as an action that does not fit the status of the person in question, and the picture becomes clearer. In the same way that moderns might react with indignation and outrage over a violation of their constitutional rights (if a police officer broke down their door and searched their house with no warrant, for example), inhabitants of a culture of honor view an expression of disrespect as an unjust violation of their status, and they react with similar indignation and outrage. While the current response to injustice typically involves lawyers, a society with a stronger connection to warrior ideals and/or frontier self-reliance tends to be more accepting of a violent reaction to insults. So while we may not agree with this hypersensitivity, we can at least understand it.

While this desire for self-directed justice may fuel the "touchy and petulant spirit" of the duelist, numerous writers have considered honor to be a powerful motivating force in the performance of virtuous actions. Cicero, for example, considered young men's desire for glory an appropriate means of shaping good character if the emphasis on justice is maintained. The best route to glory, Cicero argues, is to make oneself genuinely worthy of glory, "to behave in such a way that one is what one wishes to be thought" (*De Officiis,* II:43). Military ethicist Peter Olsthoorn's consideration of the role of honor in military contexts is a modern example of this line of thought. Humility and self-sacrifice may be considered a higher form of moral living than self-advancement, but pride has its uses, so long as it is aligned with the principles of justice, so that the warrior actually acts to become worthy of the desired glory.

The treatment of military honor provided by Ted Westhusing provides an opposing perspective. Throughout the history of Western civilization, the notion of honor as a reflection of social status has been countered by an emphasis on honor as personal morality. The anonymous 16th-century treatise *Institucion of a Gentleman* distinguishes between honor derived from social status (whether one's family is noble or peasant) and honorable character, advancing the claim that only those with honorable character are true gentlemen, regardless of high or low birth. In the mid 19th century, William Grayson satirically described the "honorable" characteristics of "gentlemen" in the American South (idleness, uselessness, frivolity, indulgence, haughtiness, drunkenness, violence, etc.), emphasizing the distinction between honor as social status and honor as internal qualities of character, available to all levels of society by virtue of the person's morality. A similar theme is found in John Ruth's Victorian-era book on etiquette, with his claim that status as a gentleman is a matter of habits and manners rather than birth and breeding.

Westhusing counters Olsthoorn's emphasis on honor as a desire for glory with an emphasis on honor as personal integrity. Integrity may be a considered a form of justice-turned-inward in which, rather than an honorable person demanding to be treated in a certain manner, the honorable person behaves in a manner that is true to his ideals. Kant's approach to ethics shifted the focus of justice away from considerations of differences in just desert, and toward considerations of universal dignity and the inherent worth of humanity. In this process, justice became less about the rules of morality derived from authority, and more about a morality involving the individual's ethical standards. Current understandings of honor as integrity have followed similar patterns of individualism and universality. Rather than honor being found in conforming to others' expectations, honor is found by living up to one's own beliefs and internalized standards of right conduct. Rather than our dignity being found in our position in society, our dignity is found in our shared humanity.

Kant considered humanity to have "unconditioned worth," and demanded that we treat all people as beings who deserve respect. That includes how we treat ourselves. When we consider that our humanity confers upon us a great dignity, we become motivated to treat ourselves in a manner that does not violate this dignity. The duty to treat oneself well is the basis for the Kantian argument against self-destructive behavior, and in favor of developing one's talents and abilities to their fullest potential.

Another consequence of our human status is that it would be beneath our dignity to behave in a manner that is less than honorable. For a being that possesses inherent nobility to do that which is ignoble is to treat the self unjustly. An honor that is based on inherent human dignity is one in which honorable persons feel an obligation to themselves, to live up to their own standards, and in so doing to achieve a sense of self-respect.

For the martial artist, this has tremendous implications. There is no social group that has historically been more focused on honor than warriors, and it is very common to see this term used by today's martial artists. So what is our honor? If honor is all about social status, then honor is how many opponents one has beaten, how many trophies and medals one has accumulated, how many people know one's name, how many people fear and respect one.

But remember that our task is to defeat our fat relentless egos. Wanting to have a bigger trophy than the other guy feeds rather than starves the ego, so defining honor as reputation is useless for a virtuous warrior. Focus more on what Cicero said about honorable actions and honorable people. We live in an imperfect world, and very often the truly honorable are pushed out of the spotlight in favor of posturing fools. Honorable actions often do not receive the public acclaim that they deserve, and honorable people often live lives of obscurity. Do the honorable thing, even if it wins no glory. "This above all – to thine own self be true." (*Hamlet*, Act One, Scene IV).

Justice Beyond the Self: Piety and Loyalty

While we were covering some definitions of justice, our examples involved the functioning of justice between individuals; the roles of uke and tori, justice toward an attacker, and so on.

This is only right, as most definitions and discussions of justice are social, rather than personal, in nature, and it is to this inter-personal form of justice that we now return. Two aspects of this side of justice will be considered: piety and loyalty.

In the dialogue entitled *Crito* (written around 360 BCE), Socrates languishes in prison, awaiting his coming execution. Crito, a friend of Socrates, comes to him with a workable escape plan. Socrates refuses. He refuses because he has been convicted and sentenced to death in accordance with Athenian law, and his conscience will not allow him to act against that law. In the dialogue between Crito and Socrates, Socrates points to the tremendous debt that he owes to Athens, comparing it to the debt between children and parents. The very laws and constitution that sheltered and guided him, provided for his education and livelihood, now demand that he die. How honorable would it be to accept only the benefits of Athens and not the cost? The "really important thing," Socrates argues, "is not to live, but to live well," and to live well requires that we act with justice. Socrates owes his life to Athens, and so he lays down his life and accepts execution when Athens demands it. While the modern mind, informed by a social contract approach to justice, recoils at characterizing the relationship between citizen and state in such a one-sided manner, this does serve well as an introductory example of "piety" as a form of justice.

The reader might feel uneasy with my use of the word "piety." Like so many virtue-related terms, the word "piety" has mutated over the centuries. Currently, when the word is used in public discussion, it is almost always used insultingly, referring to someone who is so obsessed with the details of their religion that they have either forgotten how to have fun and enjoy life, or have fallen into the trap of judgmental self-righteousness. Like honor, piety is a very misunderstood word. In this book, we will be working with the original definition and use of the word "piety," which can be understood as a form of the virtue of justice.

Working from the perspective that justice involves giving to people that which they are due, piety takes this idea and applies it to larger social units such as family, country, and religion. While most forms of justice between persons involve satisfying obligations, piety involves obligations that can never be satisfied. Can any act of service really "pay back" our parents, canceling out the debt that we owe them for giving us our lives? While modern social contract theory maintains that it is possible for a government to behave so unjustly that it violates its side of the agreement, on the positive side, what act of patriotic service finishes our obligations toward the nation under whose protection we live? For those of us who operate within a theistic worldview, at what point can creature and Creator be "even?" When does a believer get to say to God: "What I have just done for you balances your act of creating the universe and letting me live in it"? The answer is clear: we are never freed from these obligations, and it would be silly to try to claim otherwise.

"A man turns his back on his family, he ain't no good." In the Bruce Springsteen song "Highway Patrolman," a man is forced to choose between duty toward the law and duty toward family. He is a patrolman, chasing down a criminal who is attempting to escape across the Canadian border. With a profound sadness, the patrolman pulls his car over and allows the criminal to get away, because the criminal is his brother.

This dilemma is similar to the "case of concealment" found in the Confucian *Analects*. In this case, a man has stolen a sheep, and his son finds out about the crime (*Analects* 3:18). Confucius states that a dutiful son is bound to place faithfulness toward family above even the law, to the extent that he should conceal the crime committed by his father. Within the Confucian tradition, this action is described as one of *hsiao* (filial piety). Filial piety requires that we act in accordance with family obligations.

The exact nature of those obligations is, of course, a matter of considerable debate. Confucian scholars A. T. Nuyen and Lijun Bi & Fred D'Agostino are among those who have given thought to the concealment case. They agree that the conflict between civic and filial obligations puts the hypothetical son in a painful situation, and that the proper (pious) answer involves acting to shield the father from capture, but to privately (and respectfully) confront the father, reasoning and pleading with him to give up criminality and act properly.

While filial piety involves giving family members the respect and devotion to which they are due, civic piety involves giving to one's country the respect and devotion to which it is due. This renders it similar to some definitions of patriotism. While some define patriotism in terms of feelings of affection toward one's country, our approach to patriotism is duty-centered, focusing on the unrepayable debt. While the case of Socrates may be an extreme one, it does bring up some legitimate points about the relationship between citizen and state. If we are obligated to render respect to our parents for taking care of us, then we have a similar obligation to the country that provides us with shelter and protection. Josef Pieper extends this idea of civic piety to include the demonstration of proper respect for those who operate in the public sector. Whether the individual in question is an elected official, a law enforcement officer, or even a government pencil-pusher, by their actions our society functions. As agents and representatives of our country, it is just that we show them respect.

When most people hear the word "piety," they think of piety as it relates to religion. Piety in religion, however, is not terribly different than the forms of piety that we just discussed. I do not expect this concept to find tremendous resonance among readers who adhere to an atheistic perspective, but it may still prove informative for those non-theists who wish for greater insight into the theistic mindset.

In the dialogue *Euthyphro*, Socrates is in conversation with the character named Euthyphro (you may have noticed by now that many of the Socratic dialogues are titled after the character who is arguing with Socrates). Euthyphro is a religious expert who is on his way to charge his own father with manslaughter (a reversal of our Confucian son). He justifies this by arguing that piety consists of always following divine law, no matter what. Socrates, who himself is facing a charge of impiety, engages Euthyphro in a discussion about whether or not such legalism is the essence of piety, and if it is not, what the essence of piety might be. Euthyphro abandons his legalistic definition under Socrates' questioning, but is unable to provide a good alternative definition. In the end, he offers a feeble excuse and retreats from the discussion.

Euthyphro attempted to connect piety to "doing that which the gods love," but failed due to several factors. For one thing, the Greek gods often argued and fought amongst themselves. What one god loved another god hated, so no consistent definition of that which is god-beloved was possible. Euthyphro's second problem is his inability to separate "doing what the gods love" from "benefiting the gods." The gods need nothing from mortals, so piety cannot involve giving them what they need.

Followers of monotheistic religions do not have to worry about Euthyphro's conundrum of trying to know what is right when there is disagreement among the gods. However, there is still the problem of whether piety involves giving to God that which God deserves, when no mortal activities actually provide anything that God currently lacks. In the Bible, we see that God considers sacrifices to be irrelevant compared to the condition of the people's hearts (Psalm 51:16-17, Hosea 6:6), and that he neither lives in temples nor needs anything from human hands (Acts 17:24-25). A biblical answer to Euthyphro's confusion is to claim that what is just is not necessarily what is *needed*, but what is *due*, and to consider religious piety to be similar to filial or civic piety. Rather than God *needing* acts of worship, pious acts are intended to be outward displays of our inward orientation toward God. In the same way that no action will even out the scales of duty between child and parent, or between citizen and state, no action ever "pays God back" for creating and sustaining the universe. Instead, worship is an activity in which honor is justly ascribed to the one who is worthy of honor.

This examination of piety as a subset of justice is all well and good as an intellectual exercise, but what relevance is there for the life of the martial artist? Carol Andreini's comparison between the heroes found in the *Illiad* (Achilles and Hector) and the *Aeneid* (Aeneas) shows that a warrior who fights for personal glory is of limited worth. While someone like Achilles may win wars, they are not well suited for life beyond the battlefield.

As I write this, I am watching a DVD set that I received for Christmas. The program centers on a group of hopefuls who wish to compete in a Mixed Martial Arts tournament. With the popularity of competitions like these, the combatants are often admired by viewers and other martial artists. Perhaps this is simply a reflection of the nature of an athletic competition, but when these martial artists talk to the camera about why they are there, and when I observe their interactions with each other, the primary motivation appears to be personal glory, with prize money as the secondary motivation. Interpersonal interactions in the contestants' shared house mostly feature selfishness, pettiness, and bragging. This maybe the result of selective editing, the producers of the show wanting viewers to see the exciting conflict and posturing rather than quieter expressions of honorable character, in which case my criticisms should be directed toward the producers rather than the fighters. But so far I see little evidence of these martial artists fighting for anything higher than their own fat relentless egos.

A proverb of the Togakure Ryu is that "the sword should be used for peace, and to protect family, country and nature." Piety, whether it is oriented toward family, country, or something transcendent, sets in the warrior's mind the idea that there is something out there that is of greater value than the self. The impious fighter is willing to risk injury and death, but only because that is the price for glory (similar to a mercenary who fights only for a paycheck). The pious fighter goes beyond that, and is willing to sacrifice his or her life for a greater cause than vanity. "It is only when the heroism of the warrior combines with [piety] and works for a goal other than individual glory—be it for the country, the family, or the gods—that anything is truly won."

In addition to the willingness to strive heroically for the goal, this commitment to a person, cause, or faith is vital to a warrior's character. Viktor Frankl, the existential psychiatrist and WWII concentration camp survivor, connects devotion to something or someone outside of the self with the realization of one's true self: "The more one forgets himself—by giving himself to a cause to serve or another person to love—the more human he is and the more he actualizes himself." Although this may sound confusing and counter-intuitive to some, self-realization comes from self-transcendence, not from self-centeredness.

In the seventeenth century, Naganuma Muneyoshi wrote that faith is essential for the samurai: "Without faith, humaneness is a mere expedient, courtesy degenerates into flattery, intelligence is decorated with deception, duty serves adventurism, and bravery deteriorates into violence and depredation. None of these are virtues."[15]

Piety is closely linked with loyalty, so much so that Josiah Royce's definition of loyalty ("the willing and practical and thoroughgoing devotion of a person to a cause") seems indistinguishable from Andreini's description of heroic piety. Loyalty might be thought of in terms of honor (defined as integrity) and piety working together. The person of honor commits to the support and defense of someone or something beyond the self, and demonstrates the personal integrity to remain true to that commitment.

Loyalty has been highly valued across history and in all corners of the world, as may be demonstrated by the severity with which disloyalty has been treated. Dante reserved the lowest circle of hell for traitors (two circles lower than the space reserved for those who commit violent murder), and history is filled with the imaginative tortures employed against those who are disloyal. Until 1814, treason was the only crime in England that carried

---

15. Cleary, 93.

the penalty of being hanged, drawn, and quartered. Treason continues to be punishable by death in the US, and countries that have abolished capital punishment (such as Canada and Australia) threaten traitors with life imprisonment.

Loyalty for a warrior is of utmost importance. Ideals of warriorhood are often formed and tempered in chaotic times, such as Japan's Warring States period, or Europe's medieval age. Asian studies professor G. Cameron Hurst points to the treacherousness of these historical periods for the reason behind loyalty's enduring prominent status in warrior codes. In such times, when life and territory are easily lost, warlords scheme and betray, and it becomes easy to adopt an attitude of looking out for oneself, knowing whom to trust is quite literally a matter of life and death.

Hagakure places dedication to one's lord as the highest possible ideal for a samurai: "If one were to say in a word what the condition of being a samurai is, its basis lies first in seriously devoting one's body and soul to his master." Inazo Nitobe similarly places loyalty at the pinnacle of samurai ethics. While Tsunetomo and Nitobe have been criticized for romanticizing and idealizing bushido (by Hurst, for one example), even their critics agree that these two scholars of bushido were right to describe the tremendous value placed on loyalty among Japan's warrior class.

Similarly, oaths of loyalty and renunciation of all treacherous ways were solidly ingrained in the ceremonies of knighthood, and one of the worst things a knight could be called was "false." In the present day, those who wish to serve as warriors and guardians in the armed forces are required to swear oaths of loyalty, although the object of those oaths may vary (in the US, for example, the oath is one of loyalty to the Constitution. In British Commonwealth nations, it is to the Queen. In Germany, it is to the Laws and the People). Loyalty may be to individuals as well as to groups. Liu's description of the Chinese *yu-hsia* includes the ideal of an individual loyalty to one's friends. In our own chaotic times, a warrior must be known as someone who can be trusted.

Justice in Interaction with Other Virtues

As we saw in the chapter on courage, justice is necessary for other virtues to function properly. Unless actions are directed toward a just cause, those actions are unworthy of being called virtuous actions. It is because justice provides such a vital guiding and directing force that many theorists, including Plato, have regarded justice as the highest of the virtues. In the *Republic*, Plato constructs a hypothetical society that mirrors the construction of the human soul. In Plato's perfect society, each individual citizen lives and works in the social role for which that individual is best suited. All parts of the community do their job, and do it well, and for Plato that is the nature of a just society. Justice in the human soul is considered to be the same. Plato argues for the supremacy of justice in that it is justice that causes all elements of the human soul to function harmoniously, each psychological doing its job and doing it well.

Royce puts forward a similar argument about the functioning of loyalty (one of the forms of justice), saying that loyalty to a cause "tends to unify life, to give it centre, fixity, stability," resulting in a "union of various selves into one life." Lawrence Kohlberg's work on moral development also places justice as the highest possible ethical principle, basing his claim on the idea that, if one resolves all moral dilemmas according to impartial rules of justice, then every requirement of morality will be satisfied. While some other writers disagree about placing justice at the top of the virtuous pyramid (as will be seen in greater detail in the chapters on wisdom and benevolence), even those who place other virtues at the top agree that justice stands high in the hierarchy.

In the same way that justice serves the other virtues, the other virtues serve justice (further supporting MacIntyre's claim that perfection in any one virtue requires perfection in all the virtues). While justice demands that we aim our actions toward the right goals, wisdom is necessary to know which goals are the right ones, and how they are to be pursued. Courage is necessary for a life of justice, providing the ability to accomplish worthy goals in the face of fear. Without courage, we fall into the error that Confucius described as seeing what is right and not doing it. Temperance protects us from committing injustice through excess or deficiency.

Treating someone as they deserve is often a balancing act, examples of which include our previous discussion of verbal justice (speaking of someone neither more highly nor more harshly than they deserve) and self-defense situations (use of appropriate force). It is easy to allow emotions to get out of control, resulting in something being said or done that is later regretted. The ability to exert self-control and to moderate emotional responses will therefore facilitate just action.

The relationship between justice and benevolence is a contentious one. In the psychological and philosophical literature, there is an ongoing debate between theorists who focus on justice as the central element, and those who focus on caring and altruism. Some see a morality based on justice, with its emphasis on rules and duty and impartial treatment, to be fundamentally different than a morality based on benevolence, with its emphasis on compassion and mercy. Some attempt to hold both forms of ethics in balance, while others attempt a reconciliation. Some argue that love can be understood within an ethic of justice, because demonstrating compassion for others is one of our moral duties, giving us, in effect, a "responsibility to love." Others argue that justice can be understood within an ethic of care, because if we love someone, we will treat that person fairly, without the need for duty-based considerations. Steering a true course between the extremes of rejecting love or rejecting duty, and finding a way to approach life that somehow maintains these two approaches, will require substantial levels of a third interacting virtue: wisdom.

Cultivating Justice in Yourself

The great majority of research on the cultivation of justice has followed the developmental approach of psychologist Lawrence

Kohlberg. Kohlberg argued that moral development centers on one's ability to reason at higher and higher levels, resolving ethical dilemmas in accordance with the principles of justice.

Like many developmental psychologists, Kohlberg uses a stage approach. In the most primitive stages of moral reasoning, decisions are approached in terms of rewards and punishments for the self, the primary question being: "What's in it for me?" As the individual begins to advance, the focus of reasoning shifts away from immediate consequences, and to a form of reasoning based on social interaction and doing what other people expect of you. Reputation ("What would the neighbors think?") and the maintenance of the social system ("law and order") become important. Moving beyond that to the higher levels of moral reasoning, the individual "transcends" the social nature of the rules,[16] and operates based on universal standards of justice such as individual rights and the inherent dignity of humanity.

Most of the work that has been done from Kohlberg's perspective has been about helping to foster moral development in others, but the principles may also be applied by individuals toward their own development. This form of moral education typically involves presenting and discussing ethical dilemmas (such as the famous "Heinz dilemma": Is it moral for a man to steal medicine that he cannot afford, in order to save his dying wife?). As an individual exercise, I would suggest that readers seek out ethical dilemmas and take the time and effort to ponder them.

Such dilemmas are typically easy to find in news sources. For example, a group of doctors in southern Ontario have recently been developing a policy for hospitals regarding the handling of patients in the event of an influenza pandemic. The team's conclusion was to prioritize patients based on the likelihood that they will survive, a decision that may mean placing patients such as the elderly and people with AIDS at the bottom of the list. Is this the right thing to do? Before you answer, take the time to calm

---

16. There is considerable debate over whether or not this is possible.

your mind and seriously consider the situation in terms of the theories of justice that we have been covering in this chapter. It is not enough to reach a decision about this dilemma, you have to be able to intelligently articulate exactly *why* you consider this to be a moral or immoral policy. Thinking through the reasoning behind one's decision is at the heart of Kohlberg's ideas about cultivating justice.

Philosopher Bradford Hadaway, combining Kant's ethical theory with the spiritual disciplines of Trappist monks, argues that becoming a person of justice requires the ability to make judgments without selfish considerations. The natural human inclination is to bias our judgments in our own favor, and overcoming that inclination requires self-control (recall our previous discussion of temperance as a facilitator of justice). As an exercise that may help to develop the kind of self-mastery needed to make unbiased judgments, Hadaway recommends an adaptation of certain monastic practices, specifically the vow of poverty. While few of us would be willing to engage in the kind of voluntary poverty found in Trappist monasticism, there are some less extreme forms that Hadaway proposed. Temporarily giving up something that one considers personally important (cell phone, weekly shopping sprees, television, internet, the use of a personal vehicle, etc.), could be considered a "moral exercise" that fosters the kind of self-renunciation that is necessary if we want to be impartial in matters of justice.

In an earlier chapter, we examined psychological research supporting the notion that thought, feeling, and behavior are locked together in a relationship of mutual influence, and talked about behavior modification as a way of assisting in the cultivation of the thoughts and feelings that are associated with the exercise of a virtue. One possible application of this principle could involve the chivalrous virtue of *franchise*, which Keen defines as "the free and frank bearing that is visible testimony to the combination of good birth with virtue." Combine this with Bertram Wyatt-Brown's description of "true honor" in terms of "the happy congruence of inner virtue with outward, public action," and the practice of *franchise* can be seen as a method for demonstrating honor. Our everyday behavior should reflect our worth, and what we have seen of Kantian thought shows that our humanity confers upon us an incomparable worth. That dignity should be reflected in the way that we stand, walk, sit, look at and speak with others.

As an undergraduate, one of my roommates was a young man who had the worst manner of self-presentation I have ever seen. Slumped shoulders, bent neck, downcast eyes, feet dragging when he walked, a voice that was equal parts mumble and whine. I would watch him walking around (I did have to share a dorm room with him, so it would have been difficult to avoid watching him), and think to myself: "that boy walks like someone who is defeated." As he interacted with people, his manner did not elicit respect. At best, people tended to do things for him out of pity. This is not the way that a warrior interacts with the world.

Chögyam Trungpa claims that "a dignified state of existence" is expressed by our posture: "when you sit erect, you are proclaiming to yourself and to the rest of the world that you are going to be a warrior, a fully human being." An erect posture, clear and level gaze, gentle and steady voice, and open expression is associated with a person who possesses dignity. By practicing this way of presenting oneself to the world, the self is being treated as someone who possesses dignity. Treating oneself in this way can result in coming to genuinely see oneself as a person who possesses dignity, and this can be an inspiration to behave honorably in the interest of maintaining self-respect.

Finally, practice justice in small things. When speaking about others, make sure to neither be a slanderer or a flatterer. Show integrity by keeping your word in minor everyday situations. For example, don't say that you'll be somewhere and then not show up because you didn't feel like it. Your mood is not as important as your honor; you said that you would do it, so do it. Demonstrate loyalty by sticking up for your friends. Show a little respect to your parents. Show respect and devotion to your country (even if you may not like some of the things that the leaders are currently doing). If you are religious, give worship where worship is due.

Cultivating Justice in Others

As mentioned, Kohlberg's thoughts on cultivating justice involve a series of developmental stages, and fostering moral growth in others typically takes the form of discussing ethical dilemmas. The basic idea is to expose students to critical thinking principles, and to encourage them to engage those skills by thinking about morality at higher and higher levels than their current stage. As an example of this approach in action, a team of researchers worked with police officer trainees, engaging them in group discussions on law-enforcement-relevant moral issues such as capital punishment, police discretionary powers, and social deviance. Instructors assisted in the discussion, rephrasing student statements and providing leading questions intended to stimulate more discussion. More in-depth thinking was encouraged by weekly writing assignments on the challenges faced in their own lives, challenges faced by law enforcement personnel on the job, and more general matters of criminal justice. The results were promising: participants demonstrated higher levels of principled moral reasoning after the sessions than an equivalent control group (who did not receive this training).

The application of these concepts to a martial arts setting is not much of a stretch. A brief study of the many stories that we find in various martial arts reveal loyalty, self-sacrifice for a noble cause, self-defense situations and the use of deadly force, challenges and duels, plots and assassinations. More than simply entertaining stories, these are opportunities for discussion, making them opportunities for moral advancement.

Harvard moral education expert Betsy Speicher used a Kohlberg-type approach to demonstrate the effects of parents' moral reasoning on the moral development of their children. The results indicated that higher levels of moral reasoning among young people were associated with higher moral reasoning among their parents. This can be applied to martial arts instructors, as they are often older than their students, and may sometimes be perceived as surrogate parental figures. Al Bandura, the eminent psychologist who created social learning theory, demonstrated that exposing children to role models who are more morally mature was effective in developing more mature moral behavior in the children, and martial arts instructors may similarly serve as influential role models. By demonstrating to students that they think in terms of higher justice both inside and outside of the training hall, instructors can inspire their students to live lives of greater justice themselves.

Discussions in the research literature on how to foster loyalty have typically been too specific for our purposes, focusing on methods for increasing commitment to a particular organization such as a specific religion or corporation. Fostering loyalty as an individual virtue, however, has received almost no attention. Josiah Royce's book does contain some suggestions which could prove useful, and which are supported by psychological research. Specifically, he suggests that children may be trained to become loyal by providing them with role models in stories of adventure, loyal characters that may be emulated. Attachments to athletic teams are also encouraged, as they provide opportunities to demonstrate team loyalty. This is especially useful for martial arts instructors who teach arts that have a strong sporting component (such as Judo or Taekwondo). And do not reward tattle-tales, as "close friendships are amongst the most powerful supports of loyalty," and tale-bearing undermines the formation of attachments between peers. Instructors are encouraged to shift the focus of their methods to keep issues of teamwork, cooperation, and fair play at the center. The "win at all costs" approach only fosters injustice, placing emphasis on the qualities of effectiveness rather than the qualities of excellence.

Conclusion

Justice is of the utmost concern for martial artists. As far back as the time of Plato, serious thought has been given to the dangers that are present when a person of power directs that power toward an unjust goal. What exactly constitutes a just or unjust goal, however, has been debated throughout history, and the few theories of justice that we have covered constitute only a small sample of the large body of literature on the subject. Readers are encouraged to explore this subject further, and to give consideration to how their own lives may be made more just.

6

Temperance

He who is slow to anger is better than the mighty;
and he who rules his spirit than he who captures a city.
Proverbs 16:32

Do not fall prey to avarice, indulgence, or egoism.
Masaaki Hatsumi

Relatively few stories exist that provide us with examples of temperance in the warrior's life. Not as dramatic as courage or as interpersonally obvious as justice, temperance is a quiet virtue, one in which power is directed inward. Often, the successes that come from exercising this virtue are found in one who heroically refuses to act, rather than one who heroically acts. Tales are rarely told of magnificent warriors and their boundless capacity to quietly self-regulate.

One exception is in Edmund Spenser's epic poem *The Faerie Queene*. First published in 1590, *The Faerie Queene* is an allegory, in which characters represent specific virtues or vices, and their activities in the story are intended to reveal some truths about the roles that these virtues play in everyday life. Spenser had originally planned to write twelve books in the epic, the main character in each book representing an important virtue, with the possibility of another twelve books as a companion series. Unfortunately, only the first six books of *The Faerie Queene* were completed before his death in 1599.

Book Two of Spenser's epic features a young knight named Guyon. Guyon is brave, he is skilled, and he is wise enough to follow the advice of his companion the Black Palmer (who represents experience, and the need for young warriors to listen to their elders), but the virtue that Guyon truly embodies is temperance. Guyon is set on a mission of righteous vengeance against the villainous Acrasia. Enchantress, temptress, and employer of sweet-tasting poisons, Acrasia seduces knights with promises of comfort and pleasure. But her lovers become her slaves, and they degenerate into mindless animals when she is through with them.

Guyon's capacity for self-control, along with guidance from the Black Palmer, empower him to overcome the dangers and resolve the problems that he faces in his quest. His emotional self-control enables him to check his anger before he attacks the falsely-accused Redcrosse Knight. Guyon restrains himself, and the matter is cleared up without violence. Mammon, god of money, attempts to distract Guyon from his quest by tempting him with wealth, and Mammon's daughter, Ambition, promises the opportunity for worldly status. Guyon sees the self-destructive nature of greed and of materialistic self-promotion, however. He resists the temptations of Mammon and Ambition, and they are powerless to prevent him from leaving their realm. Mammon's last temptation is to offer his daughter, who is a powerful and beautiful goddess, to be Guyon's wife, but Guyon lacks the overreaching pride seen in so many warrior heroes. He refuses the offer, claiming that a mere human is not fit to take a goddess for a bride (perhaps Guyon had read enough of the Greek myths to know what tends to happen to mortals who become entangled with gods and goddesses).

With the Black Palmer's aid, Guyon proves himself to be stronger willed than Odysseus. Unlike the hero of the *Odyssey*, Guyon sails past the tempting siren-songs of the mermaids, needing neither binding nor earplugs. Finally reaching Acrasia's "Bower of

Bliss," Guyon sees through the illusion of her beautiful garden, and knows it to be a deadly trap. When taken to excess, pleasure and comfort produce weakness and slavery. Refusing to succumb to her poisonous charms, Guyon destroys the garden and frees her latest victim, the Verdant Knight. Defeated and chained, Acrasia is led away to imprisonment.

Defining Temperance

The temple of Apollo at Delphi reportedly had two phrases carved into its walls: "Know thyself," and "Nothing in excess." These maxims are connected in the Greek virtue *sophrosune*, which is commonly translated into English as "moderation" or "temperance." In the CSV, temperance is classified as the category of "positive traits that protect us from excess," but the philosophical literature on temperance provides a broader definition. Josef Pieper's treatment of temperance as a virtue centers on the ordering of one's life in accordance with the principles of reason. In this approach, the person does not merely engage in self-restraint (a definition of temperance that conjures up images of a tight-lipped abstemious killjoy), but understands the correct balance of laughter and sadness, work and play, firmness and gentleness, that characterizes the ideal person. One who is intemperate engages in a "perversion of the true through excess or underdevelopment."

The guiding principle of this virtue is "neither too little nor too much." This definition of temperance is reflected in Spenser. In *The Faerie Queene*, Guyon and the Black Palmer visit a castle ruled by three royal sisters. These sisters represent temperance and intemperance. One sister, Perissa, is intemperate through excess, stuffing herself with meat and wine, obnoxiously laughing without control, and cheating on one lover with another. The other sister, Elissa, is intemperate though austerity. She finds no joy in food or drink, refuses love, and faces the world with frowns and scowls. Between the two is Medina, striking the virtuous balance between the two vicious extremes of excess and deficiency. At this point in the story, Guyon had been entrusted to find a home for an orphaned baby, and Medina's well-developed character makes her worthy to raise the child.

Varieties of Temperance

Humility

Humility is the application of temperance to one's self-image, involving a temperate balance between excess and deficiency in self-esteem. In our current society, we are often told to pursue higher levels of pride, and we are told that our problems will be solved if we can just have more self-esteem.[17] This makes humility and modesty troublesome topics, prone to misinterpretation. Philosopher Julia Driver, for example, describes modesty as the underestimation of one's own worth, making it an exercise in ignorance. Renowned psychologist Ed Diener found high self-esteem to be the strongest predictor of subjective well-being, researchers Shelley Taylor and Jonathon Brown caused a considerable stir in the psychological community when they claimed to have found evidence that having an unrealistically high opinion of oneself is necessary for proper mental health, and televangelist Robert Schuler based his ministry on the notion that all God's children can achieve the good life by abandoning guilt, eradicating low self-esteem, and cultivating pride.

But high self-esteem is not all it's cracked up to be. Several researchers have criticized Taylor and Brown's claims, pointing out the weakness of the evidence in favor of positive illusions, and presenting evidence that unrealistic self-enhancement is associated with poor social skills and psychological maladjustment, not with mental health. People who put forward an unrealistically positive image can do better at creating a favorable first impres-

---

17. One of my favorite episodes of the fantasy TV show "Angel" featured a children's program in which puppets sang that "self-esteem is for everybody." The puppets turned out to be soul-sucking demons. Given my stand on self-esteem and humility, this makes the episode especially enjoyable for me.

sion, but it doesn't last. After a little while, the initial charm wears off, and the long-term effect is negative. High self-esteem also characterizes some people whom we would never consider paragons of psychological adjustment, such as teenage gang leaders, racists, and terrorists.

Reviewing the results of studies on the connections between self esteem and school performance, job performance, physical health, aggression, relationship quality, and happiness, social psychologist Roy Baumeister concluded that the effects of self-esteem are few, limited, and not all good. We would be better off, Baumeister argues, focusing on assisting people in doing something that makes them genuinely worthy of high self-esteem, rather than artificially boosting self-esteem to unrealistically high levels.

If this is the case, then that gives the martial arts a solid advantage. Instructors often list self-esteem as one of the benefits of training, often in the hopes of convincing parents to send their children for classes. Students can derive a realistically-high level of self-esteem by being pleased with their growing skill as they progress. Self-esteem can be a useful concept, provided we treat it as an effect, rather than a cause, of proper psychological functioning, and provided that it does not become "puffed up" into unrealistic egotism.

So having an elevated opinion of oneself is not psychologically beneficial. Is developing humility preferable? That depends on your definition of humility. Some of the definitions of humility that we often encounter do not appear promising. Norvin Richards claims that relying on the dictionary's definition makes humility seem to be synonymous with excessively *low* self-esteem. Psychological researcher June Price Tangney agrees, as her review of common definitions indicates the meaning of humility to be "holding oneself in low regard." These approaches to humility present considerable difficulty, especially given our recent survey of Kantian ideas regarding humanity's inherent dignity. But are these definitions of humility accurate? Is Driver correct in making humility out to be the possession of an unrealistic *under*estimation of oneself?

The majority view among virtue theorists is that the "low self-esteem" definition of humility is incorrect. Reviewing the philosophical, theological, and psychological literature on the topic, Tangney offers this summary of the real key elements of humility:

- accurate assessment of one's abilities and achievements (*not* low self-esteem, self-deprecation).
- ability to acknowledge one's mistakes, imperfections, gaps in knowledge, and limitations (often vis-à-vis a "higher power").
- openness to new ideas, contradictory information, and advice.
- keeping of one's abilities and accomplishments—one's place in the world—in perspective (e.g., seeing oneself as just one person in the larger scheme of things).
- relatively low self-focus, a "forgetting of the self," while recognizing that one is but one part of the larger universe.
- appreciation of the value of all things, as well as the many different ways that people and things can contribute to our world.

This definition of humility shows it to fit very well within the virtue of temperance, as a person's view of himself is brought into the moderate range between excess (unrealistically high) and deficiency (unrealistically low). However, human nature being what it is, chances are that bringing one's self-image into a realistic balance will be a deflating experience.

A recurring theme in social psychologists' research into human nature is our tendency toward overly-prideful assessments of ourselves and our accomplishments. Headley & Wearing, for example, found that 86% of participants self-rated their job performance as being above average, while only one percent rated themselves as below average. The "average person" believes himself to be an above-average driver, to be more moral than the average person, and to have a brighter-than-average future ahead of him.

We tend to attribute successes in life to our own abilities, but believe that failures are someone else's fault, and when we are members of a team that performs well, public displays of humility and team spirit usually mask the belief that our contributions to that success outweigh those of our teammates. We really are less impressive than we like to think that we are. Baumeister and colleagues, examining average self-esteem rates in American society, argues that "the pursuit of accurate self-esteem might well entail lowering self-esteem more than raising it." So while the definition of humility is not the one-directional lowering of one's self-image, the everyday functioning of humility will most likely end up being aligned with Richards' claim that to be humble is "to resist temptations to overestimate oneself and one's accomplishments."

Many martial arts instructors lament over a phenomenon called "Green Belt Syndrome," in which a student acquires a small amount of competence and suddenly develops an illusion of invincibility. Obnoxious swaggering, overconfidence, and an unteachable spirit ensues, until the student learns a (possibly painful) lesson in the true extent of their inexperience. After that lesson in humility (assuming the student does not quit out of frustration), they regain a willingness to listen and learn rather than speak, and they resume the slow upward climb of training. A temperate view of oneself may sting, but a true self-image will be of much greater usefulness to a warrior who is dedicated to improvement.

Self-Control

The second major form of temperance to be considered here is self-control. In the research literature, the terms "self-control" and "self-regulation" are often used interchangeably, defined as "the exercise of control over oneself, especially with regard to bringing in the self into line with preferred (thus, regular) standards." This control over the self enables people to achieve their purposes, and it extends to the way that we think, the way that we feel, and the way that we behave.

When self-regulation is functioning in the way that it is supposed to function, we notice when there is a discrepancy between our current actions and our goals, and adjustments are made in order to "stay on track" and achieve that goal, whether that change involves alteration of your thought processes (such as staying focused on a topic of study), emotional reactions (such as staying calm during a confrontation), or overt behaviors (such as sticking to an exercise regimen). Self-control has been shown to empower the achievement of personal goals, to assist in handling interpersonal difficulties, and even to help us deal with the fact of our inevitable mortality.

High levels of self-control are associated with academic achievement, fewer reports of mental disorders, better relationships, and a greater sense of personal responsibility. This type of self-directed strength is associated with such a large number of positive outcomes, and the lack of this strength is associated with so many negative outcomes that some scholars argue that self-control should be considered the supreme virtue. Vohs & Baumeister claim that "nearly every major personal and social problem affecting large numbers of modern citizens involves some kind of failure of self-regulation," and they point to the role that a loss of self-control plays in alcoholism, cigarette smoking, drug addiction, obesity, eating disorders, financial difficulties, violent crime, emotional problems, many health problems involving diet and exercise, underachievement in work and school, procrastination, sexually-transmitted diseases, unwanted pregnancy, and attention deficit/hyperactivity disorder.

The idea that self-control is useful to students of the martial arts should be thoroughly uncontroversial, especially for those who agree with Dave Lowry that the primary goal of martial training is self-mastery. Those who follow in the martial ways face challenges of self-regulation in all aspects of their training. Physical self-control is necessary for the correct execution of techniques, especially as one's body adjusts to moving in a new way as the instructor corrects posture, footwork, center of balance, and the many other details that compose even the most fundamental of movements.

Attention to such detail requires mental self-control. Students typically enter into martial arts training with visions of flashy moves, cinematic fight scenes, and intense action. Slowly and deliberately moving through yet another footwork drill, or painstakingly practicing a basic punch, requires mindful focusing of one's mental resources in the face of boredom and distraction.

To gain a fuller understanding of their art, students also frequently find themselves engaged in the study of topics such as history, philosophy, and foreign languages during the course of their training. Discussions of Tokugawa domestic policy, or the influence of Pythagorean mysticism on Thibault's system of fencing, require mental effort, especially for martial artists who may not be very academically-inclined to begin with.

Such physical and cognitive tasks often result in the need for emotional self-regulation. Discouragement is common as training progresses, with possible sources of frustration ranging from a current inability to get a specific technique right, to the perception that one has "plateaued" and is not making any more progress, to the difficulty of certain Asian philosophical concepts to the Western mind.

When it comes to emotional self-control, sparring sessions are veritable war zones. An arrogant posture or out-of-control attack by one's opponent can arouse anger. A powerful or skilful move by one's opponent can elicit feelings of inferiority and despair. An indicator of weakness or lack of skill by one's opponent is a temptation toward overconfidence. Patterns of reactions such as these may, in fact, be deliberately induced by the opponent in an attempt to disrupt your emotional self-control (especially if the opponent has recently been reading Sun Tsu), and battles may be won or lost based on which combatant possesses the greatest emotional self-discipline.

Temperance in Interaction with Other Virtues

As mentioned earlier, Aristotle's *Nicomachean Ethics* contains the well-known "doctrine of the mean," the principles that true virtue is often found in between two extremes, and that the extremes are vices of either excess or deficiency. Courage, for example, is the balance between cowardice and recklessness. Given the enduring impact of this principle, it is unsurprising that a virtue that protects us from excess and deficiency is considered by some to be the supreme virtue. Baumeister and Exline argue in favor of describing self-control as the "moral muscle" underlying all virtuous actions, and students of Cistercian spirituality make similar claims about humility.

Self-control makes justice possible, as conforming one's actions to principles of equity and just desert requires overriding selfish impulses, and the tendency to overestimate one's own worth. Wisdom involves the knowledge of the goal toward which we should strive, and the best methods for pursuing that goal. That knowledge, however, will not see application if the will is not strong enough to keep the person on-track, resisting the temptation to veer off in one direction or another. In an earlier chapter, it was proposed that the cultivation of calm responses to frightening stimuli could be a method for assisting in the development of courage. The usefulness of emotional self-control in the conquering of fear is obvious.

Among Cistercian monks, humility is considered the single greatest tool for self-mastery. The preeminence of humility in Cistercian thought can be clearly seen in the 12th-century writings of Bernard of Clairvaux. Bernard put forward the idea that cultivation of the spirit begins with accurate self-knowledge, and that accurate self-knowledge required an acknowledgement of our low and inferior status when compared against God, and when compared against the moral ideals toward which we strive. This deflating of self-esteem may be a "bitter and purging" experience, but it counteracts pride, which Bernard considered the root of evil.

Take a moment to examine the many ways that an unrealistically high opinion of ourselves acts against every virtue, and this approach becomes easier to understand. It is an act of courage to place oneself in danger for the sake of a just cause, but pride tells us that no cause is worth our own life. Better to let others die than to risk the all-important self. Humility therefore assists in the cultivation and expression of courage.

Interpersonal justice has been described in terms of treating people as they deserve, and in maintaining the supreme worth of humanity. Our tendency to overrate ourselves counteracts this virtue, as we begin to see ourselves as worthy of more than we truly deserve. Others, seen as our inferiors, are not treated with appropriate dignity.

Wisdom is necessary to know what cause is just, and what goals are worth pursuing. Pride distorts our perception of goals, based on whether or not those goals serve our desires and our excessive estimate of what we deserve. The touchy spirit of the duelist mentioned in our examination of honor is one result of this. Believing oneself to be far too important to stand for an insult, fights may be entered into because of a bruised ego. And once the fight has begun, arrogance is a common cause of errors in battle.

Examples of how pride confounds the warrior's life could be multiplied, but I will leave this offering as it is, and encourage readers to continue examining themselves and their actions for the detrimental effects of unrealistically high self-esteem.

These examples should be sufficient to demonstrate the importance of temperance as a virtue. Although a quiet and inwardly-directed form of moral strength, temperance is necessary for the functioning of the other strengths.

Cultivating Temperance in Yourself

The authors of the CSV, surveying the literature on humility and modesty, find no empirically-verified methods for enhancing this character strength. They suggest, however, that helpful suggestions may be found in monastic spiritual practices. The writings of Bernard of Clairvaux may again be of use to us, as he provides a series of exercises for conquering pride. Three steps of truth are prescribed: (1) knowing oneself, (2) knowing one's neighbor, and (3) knowing God.

(1) Knowing oneself: Knowing oneself involves the pursuit of accurate self-knowledge. As previously mentioned, we are not as great as we tend to think that we are, and Bernard's prediction is that a fully-accurate examination of our many weaknesses and failings will lead to greater humility. That humility will then manifest itself in greater compassion and mercy, for we will not presume to see ourselves as superior to our fellow humans. Students of the martial arts should balance their happiness over their advancing skill with an awareness of how far they still have to go.

(2) Knowing one's neighbor: Reflecting on the failings of those around us may also lead to a more realistic view of our shared humanity. Despite what has previously been said about humanity's inherent dignity and value, we are often foolish and cruel creatures.

Many people are familiar, for example, with the obedience research of Stanley Milgram. Like many others, Milgram was horrified at tales of Nazi war crimes. The tortures, the concentration camps, the gas chambers. How could seemingly normal human beings do such things? In an attempt to address questions such as this, Milgram constructed an elaborate simulation. He lied to his participants, convincing them that they were taking the role of "teacher" in a learning experiment. Participants were given control of a device that would administer increasingly-intense electric shocks to a "learner" whenever that person made an error in a memory task. As the shocks became more intense, the "learners" began shouting, then screaming in pain, complaining of a heart condition, demanding to be released, pleading to be released. As the shocks increased, so did the frantic cries of the "learner," until eventually, the screams fell silent. In reality, no shocks had been delivered. Milgram tricked his participants into believing that they were torturing someone into unconsciousness, maybe (in light of the "learner's" claims of heart trouble) to death. While this research raised numerous issues, one of the most disturbing was the number of participants who refused to obey Milgram's order to continue the torturous shocks. Out of 40 participants, only 14 refused to continue. Almost two thirds of the participants went all the way, shocking someone into unconsciousness for no reason other than the fact that Milgram told them to. More disturbing is the fact that, when Milgram repeated the experiment, this time modifying the procedure so that the participant was asked to order someone *else* to administer the electric shocks, the obedience rate jumped to over 92%!

What has this to do with cultivating humility? Consider this: of all those who are reading this book right now, the odds are almost two to one that you would have been one of those who willingly engaged in torture for no other reason that the fact that an authority figure said so. And nine out of ten of us would pass along an order to have someone else tortured. That's human nature. That is what we are. Contemplate this truth, and it may help to deflate an excessively high opinion of the species. While humans may have an inherent dignity and worth, sometimes we can be vile creatures.

This focus on human failing is meant to be an method for the cultivation of personal humility, not an excuse to gossip about the specific failings of other people. Rabbi Joseph Telushkin dedicates a sizeable portion of his *Code of Jewish Ethics* to the form of malicious gossip known as *lashon hara* ("evil tongue"), and points out that focusing on someone's failure to conform to your moral code, instead of cultivating humility, cultivates a sense of superiority. To counteract this, remember to maintain the collective "we" emphasis in your considerations of human evil, making sure not to exclude yourself.

(3) Knowing God: Contemplation of God is intended to develop humility by comparison. The psalmist asked: "When I consider your heavens, the work of your fingers, the moon and the stars,

which you have set in place, what is man that you are mindful of him, the son of man that you care for him?"

Set against an infinite deity, with the power and knowledge to create the entire universe, an accurate assessment of humanity is a very low one. This comparison may work wonders for those who hold to a theistic religion, but can this principle be made useful to those who do not believe in God? Gerber puts this principle to work in a contemplation of nature. From the delicate wonder of a dragonfly's wings to the awesome spectacle of the starry skies, one way to overcome our tendency toward self-absorption is to cultivate an appreciation for the greatness, beauty, and intricate complexity of nature. Iris Murdoch makes a similar claim about an appreciation of art. To truly appreciate beauty, it is necessary to stop thinking so much about ourselves, and start thinking about the qualities of the beautiful object.

Shifting our field of vision one further step earthward, Norvin Richards takes a step toward humility by comparing his own scholarly work to the great achievements of history's geniuses:

> Suppose, for example, that you have just had an article accepted by a leading journal. You've never been successful there before. In fact, this is much better than you ever did, earlier in your career, and as you think of your progress you are pleased. There are other ways to look at things, though. How does your work compare to what your other colleagues are doing? To the work of contemporaries at similar institutions? To that of leading philosophers of the day? To the Nicomachean Ethics, or the Theory of Descriptions? ... It isn't *that* good, and so you would be overestimating it (and, yourself), if you were to act as if it were.

This perspective can be applied in a martial arts setting by comparing ourselves against the great masters. In addition to historical writings about the accomplishments of great warriors, video exists of more recent masters of the martial arts. Many people collect these videos as a means of study, and this is a perfectly valid reason to do so. But these videos can also be put to use in counteracting tendencies of excessively-positive self-estimation. Watching masters and legends at work can remind us that we still have very far to go in our training.

Humbling exercises such as menial chores or seeking forgiveness when in the wrong may be of use in working against our tendency toward self-enhancement. Bernard of Clairvaux wrote within the tradition of St. Benedict, whose Rule for monastic life includes methods for the conquering of pride and the cultivation of humility. While some of the methods listed are not employable outside of a monastery, and some are entirely inappropriate during martial arts training (especially the method of keeping one's eyes fixed on the ground), others may be employed in our personal lives and, in the context of training, toward the cultivation of a humble attitude.

Benedict described "prompt obedience" as the first step to humility. The disciple lowers himself, acting in accordance with the superior's will instead of his own will. This principle may clearly be seen in martial training. Obedience to the teacher's instructions is vital to properly learning the art, and so nothing will be learned by those who think so highly of themselves that they rebel against the teacher's authority.

Along similar lines, nothing is learned by those who will not close their mouths. Benedict follows up his chapter on obedience with a chapter on the value of silence. Consider this quote from Benedict's Rule, and see if it does not ring true for a student of the martial arts: "The master, indeed, should speak and teach: the disciple should hold his peace and listen." A parallel saying making the rounds in martial arts circles is "Shut up and train."

Franciscan friar Nivard Kinsella offers several other possible methods for the cultivation of humility. One is to willingly undertake humiliating tasks. There are several training halls that already incorporate this approach, requiring students to sweep the dojo floor, take out the garbage, or perform other janitorial duties. This may have the benefit of keeping a student humble, knowing that vacuuming a carpet is not too low a task for such a great fighter. To work on cultivating humility in yourself, do not try and dodge these tasks, but willingly seek them out. Look for ways to help out your instructor, especially if it involves something that you would rather not do. Not only will you be developing a more humble attitude, but you will also be making the instructor's life considerably easier.

In martial training, failures are inevitable. Nobody will win each and every fight, and nobody gets techniques perfect on their first try. Friar Kinsella recommends that we admit errors freely, with a willingness to laugh at ourselves when we do something silly (which we inevitably will at some point).

Another recommended method is to try to be unaffected by praise. This is a difficult one, especially in martial arts circles, with the proliferation of belts, patches, medals, titles, and trophies available. Far too many become enamored of the idea of having the term "Master" attached to their name, or being able to brag about their black belt status to those outside the martial arts. This aligns well with Kinsella's assertion that humility is especially important for those in authority, given the additional temptation to pride that comes with status. One tip he suggests is to never call it "my" authority, because it is a gift, and a gift that must be used to serve others. A number of martial arts instructors already do this, focusing on themselves as channels of the teachings and traditions of their art, and not as anything terribly special in and of themselves. Considering oneself to be a servant has a long tradition in warrior cultures (the word "samurai" is said to be derived from a Japanese word for servant), and is key to a warrior's proper mindset.

Beginning in the late 1990s, researchers at Case Western Reserve University began collecting evidence that our ability to control ourselves appears to operate like a muscle. After exerting self-control, participants were temporarily weakened, performing less well on subsequent self-control tasks. Whether the task involved physical, mental, or emotional self-control did not seem to matter, controlling the self in one domain tired participants' self-regulatory "muscles," affecting self-control abilities in the other domains.

One application of this research to the functioning of temperance in one's life is to be aware of the limited nature of this self-control resource, and so not to attempt to do too much at once.

Muraven, Tice and Baumeister bring up the example of New Year's resolutions. How many of us have started the new year with an extensive list of self-improvement projects (lose weight, stop smoking, exercise better financial self-control, finally finish writing that book, etc.), only to see them all fail? If self-control relies on a finite source of strength, then it may be more prudent to attempt just one such project at a time. Stop smoking this year, and then wait until that task is completed before moving on to the next "project."

One possible application of this principle to martial arts training is to focus on improving one aspect of your performance at a time. "Today," you may tell yourself, "I am going to focus on maintaining good posture when executing all my techniques." It may be the case that your footwork, breathing, balance, timing, distance, or other aspects of technical excellence also require improvement, but if this research is any guide, trying to improve everything at once could result in failure to improve anything at all. Focus on posture today, focus on breathing tomorrow, and so on.

Another implication of this so-called "muscular model" of self-regulation is that, just as a muscle is temporarily weakened after it works, but eventually grows stronger after repeated exercise, one's ability to self-regulate grows stronger with practice. Psychologists Muraven, Baumeister, and Tice worked with students to improve their physical, emotional, and mental self-control. Students were assigned to one of three self-regulation exercises: one group was asked to focus on maintaining good posture, one group was asked to attempt to improve their emotional state whenever they detect themselves slipping into a bad mood, and one group was asked to keep a diary of what foods they ate (forcing them to pay attention to something that they would not normally pay attention to, thus exercising their mental control). The participants did these exercises every day for two weeks. Those students who conscientiously performed the self-control exercises showed less depletion when they performed a physical self-control task.

More recently, Baumeister, Gailliot, DeWall, and Oaten reviewed several studies on the use of deliberate interventions to increase self-control. Self-control-increasing interventions include adhering to a program of regular physical exercise, money management training, academic study training, deliberate use of one's non-dominant hand (right-handed people used their left hand, and left-handed people used their right hand) to perform a number of everyday activities (brushing your teeth, stirring drinks, using the computer mouse, carrying items, eating, and opening doors), and verbal self-control (avoiding profanity, speaking in complete sentences, saying "yes" and "no" instead of colloquialisms such as "yeah" and "nope," and refraining from beginning sentences with the word "I"). All of these methods were demonstrated to produce improvements in self-regulatory strength, supporting the notion that everyday exertions of self-control can have a cumulative positive effect.

Deliberately applying techniques such as this to one's own life can be easily visualized. Martial artists often employ daily exercises meant to toughen various body parts, increase flexibility, or improve dexterity. Adding self-control exercises to the list can be a way of strengthening the virtue of temperance.

This recent research into daily exercises aimed at increasing self-control has caused me to take another look at the insights of the abandoned tradition of "faculty psychology." Faculty psychology was a dominant theoretical approach in European and early American psychology from the seventeenth through early twentieth centuries. This approach centered around the idea that the human mind possesses several "powers" (memory, will, perception, etc), and that each of these faculties could be strengthened through exercise, in the same way that a muscle is strengthened.

Faculty psychology was eventually jettisoned from mainstream psychology due to philosophical problems involving free will, and faculty psychology's association with the discredited practice of phrenology, but the recent research by Baumeister and colleagues shows that there might still be something worth looking at here. Consider the self-control exercises described by Baumeister, Gailliot, DeWall, and Oaten (posture, using the non-dominant hand, etc.), and the impact of those exercises on self-regulation tasks, and compare those exercises with the following statement from 1916 by faculty psychologist E. Boyd Barrett: "will-power is built up by a gradual process of practice on the smallest things... every act of self-conquest in one sphere of life makes the battle easier in all the other spheres."

Possibilities that Barrett describes include keeping things tidy, exercising, getting up early in the morning, occasionally going without food, refraining from talking, performing unpleasant or tiresome chores, carefully speaking the truth, and striving for excellence in one's area of specialization.

Barrett also recommends a program of daily five-to-ten-minute will-power exercises, rotating from one to another about every ten days, so as to avoid making them automatic (and thus no longer requiring an exertion of will). The following is a list of selected exercises from Barrett's book:

1. stand on a chair with arms crossed
2. hold arms upstretched vertically
3. walk back and forth in a room, deliberately touching a specific series of objects
4. keep the eyes steadily fixed on a small object
5. submerge one hand in a bucket of cold water
6. count and recount aloud a collection of small objects
7. read a paragraph aloud forward and backward
8. write out, slowly and carefully, the sentence "I will train my will" fifty times
9. draw parallel lines
10. count aloud to 200

The tasks on this list may strike the reader as nothing more than tedious meaningless wastes of time, but it may help to consider them as psychological equivalents of doing push-ups. Nothing is really accomplished by a push-up, but the point of the exercise is the exertion itself, and the resulting long-term increase in strength.

Another possibility for martial artists is daily practice of drills, *kata,* or other components of the training. They are repetitive (sometimes tedious) activities that require effort and focus to do them correctly, so they parallel the exercises described by Barrett. Hopefully, if such activities are a part of one's training regimen, it is something already being done as a way of increasing in skill, and so knowing that one also increases one's capacity for self-control is an added bonus. If daily practice of your martial art has not yet been established as a component of your daily routine, this provides one more reason to start.

If long-term benefits can be obtained through the application of both classic and current psychology of the will, is there anything that we can learn from psychologists that can help in the short term? Certainly. Most specific situations that require self-regulation involve the ability to delay gratification, and to adjust behavior so that it moves us toward our goals, both of which have been the topic of psychological research.

The term "delay of gratification" refers to a person's choice to resist the temptation of a short-term benefit, with the understanding that the choice will lead to a greater benefit later on. Real-world examples of this principle abound. In lectures to my psychology students, I often use the entire practice of education as an example of delay of gratification. Students could easily drop out of school and take up a low-level unskilled position ("Would you like fries with that?"), which would result in short-term monetary benefits. But the fact that they are enrolled in a degree program at a university, with the accompanying financial burden, the drudgery of studying and preparing papers, the negative impact on their social lives, and the unhappy necessity of the occasional early morning class, shows me that they anticipate their degree paying off at some point in the future. The future payoff is expected to be worth the short-term costs.

Failure in tasks that require resistance to the allure of short-term pleasures can sometimes have more serious consequences than just a trade-off of greater versus lesser benefits. The short-term pleasure of illicit drug use can result in serious long-term damage. The short-term pleasure of promiscuous sexual activity can result in the long-term detrimental effects of various diseases. The short-term pleasure of criminal activity (such as theft), and the short-term rewards (free stuff), can result in a long-term prison sentence.

Columbia University professor Walter Mischel is well known for his research into the ability to delay gratification. The classic research design in Mischel's studies involves the use of children as participants. These children are offered the option of either waiting for a larger treat or immediately getting a smaller treat (two cookies later or one cookie now). The amount of time that the children are able to resist the temptation of the immediate lesser treat is taken as an indicator of their willpower. Some children easily wait the entire time period, while others try to wait but "break" part-way through. Why do some children make it while others do not? I will focus on just a few of the lessons that can be learned from examining the factors that helped the children delay gratification.

One lesson from an early study in this area is "try not to think about it." Distraction worked wonders for children's ability to resist the temptation of the short-term cookie. The researchers remarked on the "simple and effective" strategies employed by successful children, most of which involved doing "almost anything" other than think about the tasty cookie. Children would sing to themselves, talk to themselves, play games, or cover their eyes (one child managed to fall asleep) to avoid looking at the source of the temptation. Proprietors of health clubs have already made good use of this principle as a way of resisting the temptation to quit an unpleasant task by placing television sets in front of the treadmills and exercycles. Focusing on the TV program permits patrons to avoid thinking about their tired legs, extending the amount of time they are able to work out. Physical fitness is a common goal in martial artist's lives. If you are trying to get into "fighting shape" but the ice cream is calling, do something that can serve as a distraction.

What you think about while distracting yourself can play a powerful role. In a follow-up to the earlier study, children were given deliberate instructions that duplicated some of these distraction strategies. Thinking about something happy made it easier for the children to resist temptation, while thinking about something sad produced no benefit. So, when looking for a short-term distraction, make it something happy. In another follow-up study, Mischel and Baker manipulated *how* the children thought about various items during this task. What they found was that instructing children to think about the snack food got in the way of their ability to resist temptation, but only when the thoughts were about those qualities that made the food tempting. For example, children who were asked to chose between eating one marshmallow now or two marshmallows later[18] tended to fail much quicker if they were told to think about how sweet and soft and chewy marshmallows are. If the children were told instead to think about the marshmallows in a more intellectual manner (the shape and color of the marshmallows, and how those qualities are similar to other objects such as clouds or balls), their ability to delay gratification nearly tripled. So temptation may be more easily resisted if one's thoughts can be focused on something enjoyable that has nothing to do with the tempting object, or if one can think about the tempting object in a "cool" and analytical manner.

Cultivating Temperance in Others

To assist students in the development of humility, modeling will clearly be a key factor. As has been discussed previously, ob-

---

18. Not all of the studies used cookies as the tempting snack food. Some used marshmallows, while others used pretzels or piles of candy.

servers will learn moral lessons by watching those in authority, and martial arts training halls are ideally suited venues for observational learning. If the instructor is a swaggering egomaniac with touchy pride, whose self-concept revolves around the number of trophies stacked against the wall, we can expect the students to adopt a similar attitude. It may be par for the course for instructors to advertise themselves by prominently displaying those five-foot trophies front and center in their dojo windows, but such displays are unlikely to foster humility either in the instructor or the students. The mindset becomes "Look how great I am. If you want to be as great as me, sign up for classes today." The same may be said of the overly-elaborate uniforms worn by some martial artists, richly adorned with stripes and patches and images of various animals, with the name of the dojo splashed across the sleeves, back, legs, and lapels. Load the students up with these kinds of ostentatious fandangles, and you should not be surprised if the ego-feeding trappings of accomplishment become excessively important in their eyes.

Above all, instructors should be humble in their everyday behavior. Show it when responding to questions. Show it in how you talk about your accomplishments. Show it by dressing simply, and by walking rather than strutting. Show it in how you deal with rude people. Show it in how you discuss other martial arts and other practitioners. Show it by seeing yourself as a servant, as one who is tasked with the responsibility of passing on the art's teaching in a faithful manner. With every action, you teach far more than you may realize.

Deliberately attempting to instill humility in students is a tricky business. A fine line must be walked. Be too generous in your praise, and you foster narcissism. But at the same time, if you are too harsh in your criticism, you will demean and discourage your students. The concept of verbal justice might help us here. If a temperate self-concept is one that avoids both excess and deficiency, then this can be helped along by speaking to students in a manner that conveys neither higher nor lower evaluations than what they deserve. It may take a great deal of practice, learning how to humble your students in the right way without humiliating them in the wrong way.

If your goal is to help foster self-control in your students, then martial artists should be pleased to know that they are already engaged in a method for enhancing self-regulation that has received empirical support. Martial training itself has been shown to be a means for cultivating self-regulatory strength. Inspired by the line of research established by Baumeister and his colleagues, Australian psychologists Megan Oaten and Ken Cheng examined the effects of sticking to a program of regular exercise on various self-regulation tasks, both in the laboratory and in real-world settings. Sticking to an exercise program requires repeated acts of self-control, and, in accordance with the muscular model of self-regulation, the repeated exertion of the will resulted in improved self-control. Not only did participants who exercised perform better at a visual attention-focusing task in the laboratory, but they also demonstrated improved self-control in the areas of stress management, emotional control, smoking, alcohol consumption, caffeine consumption, household chores, healthy eating, attendance to commitments, spending habits, and study habits. Martial arts training often includes an exercise component, and can therefore be predicted to similarly facilitate strengthening of the will.

Even more specifically, psychologists Kimberley Lakes and William Hoyt looked at the effects of martial arts training on participants' self control. This study involved a school-based Taekwondo program. Over 200 elementary school students took part in this study. Half of the participants were assigned to a four-month program of training based on Moogong Ryu Taekwondo, while the other half engaged in standard physical education classes. Compared to the standard phys-ed group, the students who participated in the martial training demonstrated improvements in their ability to control their thoughts and emotions, in performance on a challenging math test, and in classroom conduct.[19] This fits well with the idea that regular exertions of self-regulation can result in an overall strengthening of one's self-control, and it shows that martial training can be even more effective than other forms of physical exercise.

Martial arts instructors may also choose to incorporate some of the techniques that I described for the cultivation of personal self-control into their curriculum. To those who only see the bold daring of a warrior, it may seem a strange thing that calm and quiet temperance should find such an easy and natural home in martial training. Warfare is a loud, chaotic thing, and popular images of warriors are often images of screaming berserkers. The ability to quietly seek the virtuous middle range between excess and deficiency, however, is not only necessary for the development of superior fighting skill, but also a key to the use of the martial arts as a vehicle for self-cultivation.

---

19. A statistically-significant gender interaction was found, with boys demonstrating greater improvements than girls. The authors discuss several possible explanations, including the possibility that the boys identified with the male instructor, and that martial training may be especially effective in fostering development in boys. Further research is called for before any definitive claims can be made.

7
Wisdom

*When you understand yourself and understand the
enemy you cannot be defeated.*
                                    Miyamoto Musashi

No weapon is sharper than mind.
                                    Masters of Huainan

In the Western tradition, the classic story of wisdom in action is that of King Solomon and his unorthodox handling of an
ancient maternity suit (1st Kings 3:16-28). Two women who lived
together, and who both had infant sons, came to the king to settle their dispute. One of the women alleged that the other had
rolled over onto her son during the night, killing him, and that
the defendant had then swapped her dead child for the plaintiff's
living child. The other women denied the allegation. Not having
access to genetic analysis in the 10th century BCE, Solomon set-
tled the matter with an inspired bit of applied psychology. He
handed down a grotesque compromise ruling, commanding that
the living child be cut in two with a sword, and each woman be
given half. While one of the women accepted the ruling, the other
begged the king to spare the child's life. She would rather see her
child raised by someone else than see him die. This reaction was

all that Solomon needed, and he immediately reversed his ruling, granting the child to the one who had revealed herself to be the true mother.

Definitions and Varieties of Wisdom

Wisdom stands alongside justice as a virtue that has been hotly debated for thousands of years, with the oldest known wisdom literature dating to a period in Egyptian history around 3000 BCE.

As discussions and debates concerning the acquisition of wisdom took on widely-varying forms, so to did the proposed definitions of what wisdom itself really is. According to historian Eugene Rice, the definition of wisdom within the Hebrew tradition was so broad that it encompassed all forms of knowledge, including King Solomon's command of botany and zoology, and the skill of craftsmen, pilots, and snake charmers. Toward the other extreme, the fourth-century heretic Arius defined wisdom so narrowly that only God could be wise, excluding the rest of us from that virtue. As described earlier, Buddhist wisdom involves the ability to see past illusion to the true nature of reality, while Confucian scholars believe wisdom to involve only an awareness of fundamental moral principles.

More recently, psychologist Robert Sternberg gathered together nineteen of the top scholars in the field of wisdom to collaborate on a book on the topic. The result included over a dozen definitions of wisdom, some of them quite divergent from each other. Psychologists from the Max Planck Institute for Human Development in Berlin, for example, proposed a program of empirical scientific research into the characteristics of wisdom, which they defined in terms of the ability to expertly apply one's knowledge toward answers to difficult life problems. Other scholars in the group disagreed with this definition. One claimed that wisdom stands apart from science, while another said that wisdom is less about one's knowledge and more about knowing the limitations of one's knowledge, and a third said that wisdom is not found in those who can answer questions but in those who can discover new questions.

What most scholars agree on is that wisdom is some form of knowledge. But what form? Classical Greek thought on wisdom often involved three categories of knowledge: *sophia* (transcendent philosophical wisdom), *phronesis* (practical wisdom, also called prudence), and *episteme* (scientific knowledge), but that arrangement was immediately disputed, and most scholars exclude scientific knowledge from their approaches to wisdom. Socrates believed that wisdom was obtained through moral development rather than acquiring naturalistic knowledge, and Plato believed that a person did not even necessarily need to be literate to be wise.

In Sternberg's research on wisdom, he found that smart people can often be very foolish. This distinction between wisdom and scholarly knowledge fits well with our everyday experience. Scientists and academics, who may be brilliant contributors to their respective disciplines, may nevertheless make silly mistakes such as falling for offers of zero-down, forty-year mortgages, and they typically do little better than the rest of us when it comes to addressing the larger questions involving the meaning of life, the universe, and everything.

In Plato's time, there was a widely-circulating joke about the philosopher Thales. The story went that this brilliant scholar was so engrossed in astronomical study that he tripped and fell down a well while staring at the stars (perhaps making Thales the original absent-minded professor). Within the Asian tradition, Confucius and neo-Confucian thinkers such as Mencius considered intellectual knowledge to be fairly irrelevant to the pursuit of wisdom. Like Socrates, they believed that wisdom is a matter of realizing natural moral principles rather than acquiring technical know-how. Leaving scientific knowledge aside as a possible form of wisdom, then, we turn to transcendent and practical wisdom.

One of my favorite paintings is Raphael's "School of Athens." Created in the early 16th century, it is a fresco adorning one of the rooms in the Vatican's Apostolic Palace. The fresco is a representation of classic philosophy, and features characters who represent great thinkers of antiquity, in animated discussion with each other. Diogenes, the Cynic who despised materialism and civilized refinement, lounges in the middle of the steps with his begging bowl. Ptolemy, the astronomer and geographer who systematized the geocentric view of the universe, holds a globe. Euclid, one of the great founders of geometry, bends down to draw a geometric figure on a tablet. In the center of this scene are two figures who represent Plato and Aristotle. It is this central section of the painting that has always drawn my attention. As Plato and Aristotle debate, their hands are pointing in different directions. Plato points upward, representing his view that truth can be found by focusing your attention toward eternal principles that transcend earthly existence. Aristotle points outward horizontally, representing his view that truth can be found by focusing your attention on the world around you.

In terms of our discussion of wisdom, those who lean more heavily toward Plato's side of the argument tend to emphasize transcendent wisdom. Plato's "vertical" approach to philosophy was firmly bound up with his view of human existence. Plato was a strong dualist, maintaining a clear distinction between the material world of flesh and the spiritual world of ideas. Platonic dualism is also hierarchical in nature, maintaining that not only are flesh and spirit distinct, but also one is clearly superior to the other. The material world is shifting and transitory. Things are never perfect, and they never stay the same. Pure ideas, however, like justice, beauty, and mathematical principles, are eternal. The laws of mathematics do not change with the weather or with somebody's mood, and justice does not grow old and die. Eternal truths do not vary from person to person or from place to place. For Plato, wisdom is knowledge of the eternal truths, and so the development of wisdom cannot rely on the material world.

When Paul Wink and Ravenna Helson conducted their psychological research into the natures of transcendent and practical wisdom, they found inner self-awareness, the ability to reconcile seemingly opposed intellectual concepts, and the search for answers to the meaning of life to be the characteristics of the transcendently wise person. People who possessed transcendent wisdom demonstrated greater openness to new ideas, intuition, and creativity.

Examples of connections between transcendent wisdom and the practice of the martial arts may easily be seen in those arts that have a connection with Ch'an Buddhism (Zen in Japanese). Ch'an/Zen stands within the Mahayana stream of Buddhist thought, which defines enlightenment in terms of the ability to see past the illusion of individual existence to know the transcendent truth that there is no separation between self and other (an example would be Bruce Lee's famous statement that when he faces his opponent, there is no opponent). This approach to Buddhism involves the employment of exercises that enable the practitioner to transcend egoism by detaching from the perception of self.

The martial arts offer opportunities for experiencing moments of selflessness by becoming totally absorbed in the activity of the moment. Bruce Lee begins his *Tao of Jeet Kun Do* by stating that "to obtain enlightenment in martial art means the extinction of everything which obscures the 'true knowledge,' the real life.'", and that "the oneness of all life is a truth that can be fully realized only when false notions of a separate self, whose destiny can be considered apart from the whole, are forever annihilated." Lee connected this enlightenment with the free-flowing formlessness of his approach to fighting.

Takuan Soho, the seventeenth-century Zen master, directly connected the study of the sword to the Zen approach to enlightenment, arguing that the detached mind brings with it strategic advantages as well as spiritual growth: "Whether an opponent attacks or you attack, if you fix your mind on the attacker, the attacking sword, the pace or the rhythm, even for a moment, your own actions will be delayed, and you'll be killed."

Because cultivating the ability to instantly respond to one's opponent so closely parallels the selfless detachment that is characteristic of Zen enlightenment, the training itself becomes a way of experiencing transcendent truth. This connection is maintained by current students of Kendo, who use their training as a method for self-cultivation through the "taming of the ego," which "prevents the mind from being swayed by external distractions, enables the practitioner to develop concentration and alertness, and provides the reflexive mechanism necessary to develop kendo skills. But more important than that is to enable its practitioners to channel that discipline to realize personal growth."

Similarly, students of *Kyudo* (archery) train in such a way that total absorption in the act of drawing the bow results in a clear mind and the inner peace that comes from selfless existence. When the self is transcended, this inner peace is extended to others. Feliks Hoff, a German Kyudo practitioner with over thirty years of experience, says that "the mind that born from practicing the Bow loves people, loves all things, it makes no distinction between things in and under heaven."

For followers of the "horizontal" Aristotelian tradition, wisdom is obtained by observing the material world, and using the knowledge conveyed by our senses to discover the basic cause-and-effect principles of the universe. The emphasis here is on practical wisdom, which MacIntyre defines in *After Virtue* as the ability to exercise good judgment in particular cases.

MacIntyre's approach to practical wisdom has had a strong impact on psychologist Blaine Fowers, who describes the exercise of practical wisdom as a three-step process. The first step is perceptive in nature, and the wise person is able to distinguish between the important and the unimportant aspects of a particular situation, seeing what is "really going on" without being distracted by peripheral issues.

The second step is deliberative in nature, and the wise person is able to determine what goals are to be pursued in the situation and how to integrate these goals with other relevant goals (for example, how to pursue career success without sacrificing family relationships).

The third step is to make a reasoned choice between different possible strategies for attaining the desired goal, and deciding how best to carry out those strategies.

When Wink and Nelson turned from their examination of the transcendently wise person to the practically wise person, they found the characteristics of the practically wise person to include good interpersonal skills, superior decision-making ability, and expertise in giving useful advice. People who possessed practical wisdom demonstrated greater leadership ability, empathy, and concern for making the world a better place.

An example of practical wisdom within the martial arts can be found in the work of the English swordmaster George Silver. In his *Brief Instructions*, published in 1605, Silver discusses the application of good judgment in the fight. "Judgment" is Silver's term for the ability to quickly perceive the distance between oneself and the opponent, the amount of time it takes to traverse that distance, what possible attacks are available from any position, and how best to make use of that information to attack and defend. Align these ideas with Fowers' description of the three steps in the making of wise practical decisions, and Silver's advice fits very well within the tradition of Aristotelian practical wisdom. A wise fighter can quickly perceive the essential elements of a situation, the goal to be attained, and the best method for the pursuit of those goals.

A similar approach can be found in Bruce Lee's description of five different kinds of speed that are desirable in a fighter: perceptual (quickly seeing openings), mental (quickly selecting the right move), initiation (having the right physical posture and mental attitude to efficiently launch techniques), performance (quickness in carrying out the move), and alteration (the ability to quickly change as the situation calls for it).

A wealth of practical wisdom can be found in Sun Tzu's classic book of strategy *The Art of War*, and a great many students of the martial arts look to this volume as a source of advice and inspiration. In it, Sun Tzu provides counsel for aspiring warlords on a wide range of variables involved with carrying out successful campaigns of defense and of conquest, including the proper handling of territory, supply lines, propaganda, spies, rewards, deception, peasants, uniform design, troop morale, and the position of the sun.

Similar to the example of Solomon, students of strategy are often drawn to Sun Tzu's use of applied psychology. He provides advice in such matters as the sowing of confusion, provoking an opponent into unthinking anger by insulting his wife, treating the enemy's warriors with respect, the establishment of an intimidating impression, and keeping one's cool in battle.

Sun Tzu's strategic advice can also be seen in terms of Fowers' approach to Aristotelian practical wisdom. Sun Tzu urges warlords to know specifically what goals are to be sought with the campaign, and to believe completely in the morality of why those goals are to be pursued; to take into account all possible factors involving one's army, one's opponent, and the territories involved in the conflict; and to strike only when all preparations have been made and when it is of maximum advantage. Once engaged, the warlord must demonstrate the resiliency to quickly adapt to changing conditions. He "moves and strikes like a poisonous snake," turning every circumstance into a path to victory.

Assuming that practical wisdom is a unitary ability, strengthened through practice and applicable in a wide range of domains in life, the martial arts become an opportunity to practice and develop this form of wisdom. This is especially useful given the rapidity with which many decisions must be made. In the same way that combat is a mercurial environment, life-altering decisions about work, family, and personal health can be made in the blink of an eye as situational factors quickly shift and flow. If increasing one's ability to rapidly perceive the truth of a situation and act accordingly has any cross-situational utility, then training in the martial arts may also be a method for the cultivation of practical wisdom.

The distinction between practical and transcendent wisdom, which I have portrayed in terms of Plato versus Aristotle, is found within Eastern thought as well. Confucian philosopher Chung-Ying Cheng claims that "wisdom is both retrospective and prospective, both inner-looking and outer-looking, both personal and communal, both historical and metaphysical, both applied and theoretical." This dual nature of wisdom as transcendent and wisdom as practical is found in the scholarly literature on Confucianism, Daoism, and Buddhism[20] as well as the literature on Plato and Aristotle, and these two principles have wrestled their way through the history of philosophy in all corners of the world. Some thinkers have tried to find a way toward a harmonious blend of the two, while others have maintained that they stand in irreconcilable conflict.

Those who, like Plato, adopt a hierarchical dualism, but do not balance it with an Aristotelian emphasis on practical wisdom, see the material world as a hindrance to be shunned or overcome in the pursuit of eternal truths. An example of this in action are the ascetic practices of certain hermits. Within the Christian tradition we have Simeon Stylites, who spent 36 years living atop a pillar near Antioch in the fifth century, while a Buddhist example might be the nine years that Bodhidharma is said to have spent staring at a cave wall in Henan Province in the fourth century. Practitioners of the Japanese martial arts may have encountered stories of *yamabushi*, ascetic warrior-monks who withdrew from society for contemplation and arduous training. All of these are examples of people and traditions in which the pursuit of wisdom involves a devaluation of the physical world in favor of the spiritual, requiring a removal of the self from society, and the harsh treatment of the flesh.

---

20. For an example, see the articles on wisdom in the September 2006 special issue of the *Journal of Chinese Philosophy*.

Moving from one extreme to the other, the work of late six-teenth-century philosopher Pierre Charron is considered by many to be the ultimate example of the Renaissance humanists' "secu-larization" of wisdom. While medieval thinkers such as Aquinas had blended the transcendent and practical forms of wisdom within a coherent system of thought, Renaissance thinkers began to conceptually disentangle these notions. These thinkers dem-onstrated a preference for temporal prudence over transcendent enlightenment: "the [transcendently] wise man lacks prudence almost by definition. He is so preoccupied with high intellectual matters that when the time comes for action he is usually ridicu-lously unprepared and inept."

Charron's treatment of wisdom entirely divorces the temporal from the transcendent, considering the latter useless while en-shrining the former in an illustration as a triumphant goddess. Charron's pictorial presentation of wisdom is a purely humanistic one, standing victoriously on a pillar, arms crossed as if embrac-ing herself, and looking into a mirror, for she needs no source of wisdom beyond herself.

Within the martial arts, practical wisdom with no transcen-dent component can be found among those whose teachings are entirely devoted to the pragmatic aspects of winning fights. The 14th-century manual on sword-and-buckler combat, known today only as Royal Armouries Manuscript I.33, is an entirely pragmatic document, as is Sun Tzu's *Art of War*. The majority of martial arts books currently on the market would also fall within this category.

The wisdom of the radical ascetic is one that fully embodies the saying that some people are "so heavenly-minded they're no earthly good." The wisdom of the radical humanist is one in which you place yourself on a pedestal, gaze lovingly into your own eyes, and give yourself a great big hug. It's my view that both of these extremes are flawed examples of wisdom.

It's common within virtue ethics to ground our understanding of character strengths in humanity's inherently social nature, and both the excessively-transcendent wisdom of the radical ascetic and the excessively-practical wisdom of the radical humanist are corrosive to communal functioning. Any devaluation of either the transcendent or practical component of wisdom results in an isolation of the individual from others. Transcendence without earthly prudence produces Plato's ascetic: cut off from humanity and lost in contemplation. Prudent practicality without transcendence produces Charron's self-absorbed humanist: socially active but unable to see beyond her own reflection. Go too far in one direction, and the wise person becomes someone who is isolated through retreat. Go too far in the other direction, and the wise person becomes someone who is isolated through narcissistic encapsulation.[21]

A balanced approach to wisdom is one in which transcendent factors provide the foundational ideas about the nature of life and humanity that inform practical concerns. In contrast to Charron's exclusion of transcendent wisdom in favor of practicality, another Renaissance thinker, Justus Lipsius, combined both aspects in his claim that "the wise man should have some ground in an elaborated philosophical system. He must be able to justify his convictions by means of an ethics which itself springs from a philosophical view of knowledge and nature."

One reason that practical wisdom cannot be divorced from transcendent considerations of ultimate value is that a wise practical decision implies that there is such a thing as a "best" solution. A "best" solution is one in which true ends are pursued in accordance with the principles of the real world, and practical wisdom consists of understanding the means toward the true

---

21. It is worth noting that, while I have characterized transcendent wisdom as Platonic and prudence as Aristotelian, neither Plato nor Aristotle themselves are representatives of either extreme. While Plato argued that true wisdom comes from a transcendence of physical reality, one of the main arguments of the *Republic* is that it is the philosophers (professional seekers of transcendent truth) who are best suited for the practical job of ruling society. Aristotle, who urged us to use our senses to determine the causal principles of the natural world, grounded practical wisdom in the ability to examine the divine metaphysical "First Cause," and declared, in his *Eudemian Ethics*, that humanity's highest good is the contemplation of God.

ends of life. Transcendent wisdom allows us to question what the real world is, and what the true ends of life are.

Robert Sternberg, in developing his "balance theory of wisdom," describes a wise person as someone who is able to apply practical problem-solving skills in such a way that the person's values are put to use balancing the demands of multiple interests and environmental factors toward achieving the common good (a definition that draws heavily from the practical side of wisdom). But what values should be brought into play? And what exactly is the common good? Sternberg has no answer, suggesting that we turn to moral philosophy and religion for these concepts, but he insists that without these concepts, wisdom is not wisdom. Tyrants and dictators, Sternberg argues, may employ practical problem-solving skills to balance environmental variables and multiple interests, but if the overall agenda is evil, then the person is not wise.

While examples have been given of martial artists whose thought reflects a preference for one form of wisdom over another, other warriors incorporate the perspective of grounding practical considerations in metaphysical principles. Zen Buddhist thought on the nonexistence of the self and the "mind of no mind" have a direct impact on tactical and technical advise found in the works of both Miyamoto Musashi and Bruce Lee, and the fencing style of 17th-century swordmaster Gerard Thibault is grounded in Pythagorean geometric mysticism.

Musashi, for example, writes his *Book of Five Rings* from a perspective that shows a strong influence of Zen thought (even though he describes himself as not being a very religious person). His advice flows directly from his study of the Zen concept of *mu* (nothingness), impacting what he has to say about non-consciously reacting to opponents, flexibility in one's grip on a weapon, fluidly shifting strategies as the situation calls for it, and avoiding rigid stances.

Hopefully, this will be an area for growth among students of the martial arts. An increase in the number of martial artists who can see and understand how practical specifics flow from fundamental principles would result in greater sophistication and depth in this area of study.

Wisdom in Interaction with Other Virtues

Sternberg's insistence that wisdom is only wisdom when it is directed toward the common good parallels our examination of the role that justice plays in the life of the virtuous warrior. In the same way that courage is only a virtue when directed toward a just cause, wisdom without a just cause is only amoral problem-solving.

The mutually-supportive nature of the virtues is further demonstrated by the fact that, while wisdom requires justice in order for our decisions to be oriented toward a right cause, justice requires wisdom so that we can see what cause is in fact the right one. The virtue of temperance is commonly associated with the ability to maintain one's behavioral orientation toward desired goals, enabling us to pursue the just cause. This places temperance in such an intimate relationship with practical wisdom that Peterson and Seligman classify prudence as a form of temperance, rather than a form of wisdom, in the CSV (I disagree with their classification, but I consider such disagreements to be an inevitable byproduct of the intertwined nature of the virtues).

Courage is necessary for the life of wisdom, as the wisest course of action will not always be the safest one. Wisdom and courage are both required for temperance to function, especially when it comes to humility, that form of temperance which brings our self-concept into the correct median between pride and self-denigration. To develop an accurate perception of oneself, courage is needed to overcome the fear that taking the necessary blow to our self-esteem is a psychological wound from which we may not recover, and wisdom is required so that we can perceive the true worth of ourselves, and thus cultivate an accurate self-concept.

Sternberg, in addressing possible explanations for why highly intelligent people can still act foolishly, develops five reasons. According to Sternberg, smart people can do extremely foolish things when they believe that (1), they are so smart that they can accomplish anything, (2) their interests are more important than others', (3) they already know everything that they need to know and have nothing more to learn, (4) their intelligence makes them invulnerable, or (5) they are clever enough to get away with anything. All five of these failings can be seen as the maintenance of an elevated opinion of oneself, making humility a necessary corrective for one who wishes to be wise.

Wisdom allows us to locate the courageous balance between cowardice and recklessness by knowing when to fight and when to run, making it of exceptional importance in the life of the warrior. George Silver's coverage of good judgment in his *Brief Instructions* includes the "twofold mind" of pressing in and flying out. Silver advocates moving in when attacking, pressing the opponent in such a way that openings are created and exploited. But the fighter must also be ready to quickly evade the opponent's attacks, and to retreat out of range when appropriate.

This twofold mind is also seen in Musashi's *Book of Five Rings*, with his advice to keep a door or other avenue of escape always behind you. While Musashi repeatedly emphasizes the importance of having the mindset of all-out relentless attack, he balances this with the idea that "there is nothing wrong with escaping from combat if you are overpowered and honestly cannot win the fight. Get out and make sure that you have provided a means to get out." Judgment is needed to maintain both mental principles simultaneously, and the rapid processing of information that is characteristic of practical wisdom allows the fighter to switch from offense to defense in an instant.

When these virtues are acting together, wisdom also comes to facilitate benevolence. As previously discussed, a humble attitude toward the self will incline us to be more charitable in our treatment of other people. We can more easily forgive, because we see that we are not quite as firmly entrenched on the moral high ground as we might like to think that we are. We are more likely to offer help, because we can see past psychological illusions such as the *just world phenomenon* (blaming the victim) the *in-group bias* (the tendency to perceive members of our own groups as superior to outsiders), and the *bystander effect* (the tendency to assume that "somebody else" will surely do something to remedy the situation), and see ourselves in the face of the one who needs our assistance.

Buddhism directly connects transcendent wisdom and benevolent activity. By developing the mindset that individual existence is illusory, Buddhists detach themselves from the notion of separation between self and other. The result is that the person feels compassion toward all creatures, the same amount of compassion toward friends, strangers, and even enemies that one usually feels toward oneself.

Due in part to this intimate interaction between wisdom and the other virtues, numerous scholars have been attracted to the idea of wisdom as supreme virtue. Among the scholars from whose work we have been drawing, Pieper, MacIntyre, and Fowers are examples of those who consider practical wisdom to be "foremost of the virtues." Wisdom allows us to know the right thing to do, and the best way to go about it. Wisdom tells us who we are and who other people are and what the world is. Aristotle's description of the ultimate form of human life is one in which our capacity for rational thought finds its fullest expression, and it is wisdom that most closely aligns with the exercise of the rational mind.

Cultivating Wisdom in Yourself

Beginning with the earliest known wisdom literature, those who want to increase their wisdom have been advised to pay attention to the lessons of those who have gone before. The most direct and effective method for this is the study of classic literature and works of philosophy. The better you are able to connect the thoughts of history's great minds to your life, the closer you come to making their wisdom your own.

However, many may find the prospect of trying to comprehend great thinkers' writings intimidating, and most of us remember times as students when we were forced to slog through a terribly dull and incomprehensible book on the argument that it was "good" for us. For those who may be hesitant to venture into ancient texts, Cambridge literature professor (and author of the beloved *Chronicles of Narnia* series) C.S. Lewis has these words of encouragement:

> I have found as a Tutor in English Literature that if the average student wants to find out something about Platonism, the very last thing he thinks of doing is to take a translation of Plato off the library shelf and read the *Symposium.* He would rather read some dreary modern books ten times as long, all about 'isms' and influences and only once in twelve pages telling him what Plato actually said. The error is rather an amiable one, for it springs from humility. The student is half afraid to meet one of the great philosophers face to face. He feels himself inadequate and thinks he will not understand him. But if he only knew, the great man, just because of his greatness, is much more intelligible than his modern commentator. The simplest student will be able to understand, if not all, yet a very great deal of what Plato said; but hardly anyone can understand some modern books on Platonism. It has always therefore been one of my main endeavors as a teacher to persuade the young that first-hand knowledge is not only more worth acquiring than second-hand knowledge, but is usually much easier and more delightful to acquire.

So if you have convinced yourself that only philosophers should read philosophy, take a lesson from Lewis. Whether your interest is Plato, Cicero, Aquinas, Confucius, the biblical wisdom literature, or the Buddhist sutras, don't be afraid to go to the source.

However, one bit of advice: try not to read them the way that we all tended to read things in school. For most of us as students, the tendency was to get as many of the facts crammed into our skulls in as short an amount of time as possible, usually with an eye toward what elements will be on the exam. This is not even the best way to study, much less the best way to become wise. Read slowly. Read thoughtfully. If that means that it takes you half a year to read Plato's *Republic*, that's just fine. It will be worth the extra time and effort. If you consider yourself to be a "visual learner," make the effort to picture yourself in the scene. If you tend to be more auditory, try to hear the words as if they are being spoken. Connect the ideas with what you already know. Do you agree with what is being said? Why or why not? Can you remember examples from your own life when you have seen these ideas operating? How might you have made a different decision in a past situation if you were operating in line with the ideas being presented? By questioning as you read, you go beyond simply "reading through" a text, and you begin "thinking through" that text.

This same approach can be applied to martial arts training. While training often involves the seemingly-endless repetition of movements and techniques, pay attention to the concepts behind the movements. Consider what you are doing in light of whatever training you have had in the past. What effect is this technique supposed to have on an opponent's body? Are there other techniques that produce a similar effect? How do variations in footwork, direction of movement, etc., change the results of a technique?

Many masters of the martial arts have taken the position that martial training is not about learning the techniques as such, but about learning what is "inside" the techniques. Techniques are specific manifestations of universal principles of the martial art, and the goal for the student is to internalize these universal principles through their practice.

This attempt to see and know the universal within the particular is common to both martial training and the study of great literature. Cross-apply these principles, and you may find that, the better you become at connecting universal principles in the statements of history's wise figures to everyday situations, the better you become at connecting universal principles of body mechanics to the particulars of martial techniques, and vice versa.

A few years ago, a trend started among young people to wear bracelets with the letters "WWJD" on them, with WWJD standing for "What would Jesus do?". The idea was that, when faced with a dilemma, a glance at the bracelet would bring Jesus and his teachings to mind. As fads often do, the WWJD fashion quickly spiraled out of control. It became common, then it became commonplace. Through overexposure, the bracelets became trite clichés that were leeched of their original meaning.

In terms of the cultivation of wisdom, however, the underlying concept is one that has received support in the scientific research literature. Researchers affiliated with the Max Planck Institute for Human Development in Berlin tested the notion that wisdom, being inherently social (as are all the virtues), would be facilitated through dialogue. They found that discussing difficult life problems with others before thinking the problems through oneself resulted in improvements in the wisdom of participants' thought processes. However, they also included an experimental condition in which they instructed research participants to spend ten minutes by themselves thinking about what someone whose opinion they value would say about the problem. Imagining what someone wise would say not only resulted in improved wisdom scores, but the effect was statistically equal to the effect of a face-to-face dialogue with a tangible person.

So, while the WWJD bracelets fade into the mists of time along with pet rocks and parachute pants, the concept remains useful. Cultivating wisdom may be facilitated by selecting a paragon of wisdom and asking yourself what that person would say to you about handling life's difficulties.

Cultivating Wisdom in Others

Based on Sternberg's balance theory of wisdom, the Teaching for Wisdom Program is an experimental educational approach that aims at assisting students in the development of the moral and intellectual abilities that are vital to the functioning of wisdom. This program was designed to be incorporated into a middle school American History course, but can be adapted for use in multiple possible topics. While the elements of this program are described in terms of the cultivation of wisdom in others, they may also be fruitfully applied by those who wish to cultivate wisdom in themselves.

Remember that Sternberg describes a wise person as one who successfully employs their values toward the common good, taking into account multiple interests and environmental factors. The interests identified by Sternberg are intrapersonal, interpersonal, and extrapersonal.

Intrapersonal interests are the desires of the person making the choice; they answer the question, "What do I want out of this situation?" There can be many answers to this question in any given circumstance, and often there will be more than one desire operating in the mind of the person, ranging from the concrete (e.g., the search for a new job may involve the desire for greater pay) to the relational (the search for a new job may also involve the desire to move to a different geographic location, one that is closer to family) to the spiritual (the desire for a new job may involve the sense that one is divinely "called" to a particular task). In some cases these desires may conflict (a job with higher pay may demand more time spent away from family), while in others they may cooperate (one may feel a sense of calling toward a position that also affords greater family contact).

Interpersonal interests are the desires of other people in interaction with the person making the choice. A wise choice cannot be an egocentric choice, and when choices are made, the effects are seldom restricted to the life of the chooser. This fits well with our previously-discussed Kantian view of justice as the treatment of people as ends in themselves, rather than as mere means to one's own ends.

Extrapersonal interests are those of the person's larger world, incorporating the goals of the community, nation, world, and God. The making of a wise choice involves bringing all of these factors together, and deciding how best to pursue a course of action that takes all three sets of interests into account.

The environmental factors proposed by Sternberg involve our range of response options when making a wise choice. These possibilities include adapting ourselves to the environment, reshaping the environment to suit ourselves, or deciding to leave in favor of a new environment. A wise choice may involve doing one of the three, or it may involve some combination.

As an example, consider the possibilities if a conflict arises between a student of the martial arts and the instructor. In this example, the student does not understand why weapons training is not available to students below the black-belt level. While some would take a hard-line stance that a student may never question an instructor, I might suggest that this attitude is insufficiently humble for an instructor to adopt. Others might push to an extreme on the side of the student, considering the instructor to be there for the benefit of the student (the student is paying for all of this, after all), but this would also be a form of egocentrism. When either of these extreme mindsets are adopted, the tendency is to approach the questioning in a confrontational manner, with the student taking the role of a dissatisfied customer or the instructor taking the role of a superior being presumptuously challenged by an ignorant inferior. A better course of action would involve a private and respectful discussion between teacher and student.

Within this example, we will focus on the ways in which the student may be wise. A wise approach to this situation, according to Sternberg's theory, would take into account the intrapersonal, interpersonal, and extrapersonal interests.

Intrapersonal interests could include the student's desire for the fun of handling a weapon, and a belief that she is ready to begin weapons training. Giving thought to interpersonal interests can involve taking the instructor's perspective: What if the instructor believes that "kyu"-level students are not ready for weapons? Presumably, the instructor knows more about the potential danger than the student does. Might the instructor be facing any legal or insurance-related difficulties by exposing students to weapons for which they might not be ready? And is the desire for weapons training sufficient reason for asking the instructor to disrupt an established training system?

From an extrapersonal perspective, what is the custom within this particular martial art? The restriction of weapons training to "dan"-level students may be formalized in the art's curriculum by a multinational organization to which the school belongs. Some consider humble submissiveness of the student to be an essential component of the martial spirit; would asking the instructor to change the training be a violation of that spirit? On the other hand, many martial arts incorporate weapons training at the earliest levels, so it may not be such a concern to at least ask for an explanation. If the instructor (who we are assuming is also acting wisely) gives the student a fair hearing, and explains why weapons training is restricted to black belt and above, the student might be willing to submit to the instructor's authority and continue the training, looking forward to the day when she is ready to hold a weapon. This would be an example of adapting to the environment. Alternatively, the instructor may decide that the student has a valid point, and begin to introduce some very basic weapons training into the curriculum. In this way, the student has shaped the environment through respectful suggestion.

As a third option, the student might decide that this is not the art for her, and may choose to leave in favor of a new environment, seeking out an art that offers the kind of training that she desires.

In the Teaching for Wisdom Program, this kind of thinking is encouraged as students explore the history curriculum. Rather than covering topics such as the Boston Massacre in terms of memorizing dates, locations, and details, students engage in group discussions in which wisdom-related concepts are applied to the topics. How did a dispute over a barber's bill result in five people's deaths? What were the Massachusetts officials hoping to accomplish with the British soldiers' trial? What differences do we see in the description of the incident in the American press versus the British Captain's written report? How did this relate to the overall state of relations between Britain and the colonies? Those who wish to incorporate wisdom training into a program of study in the martial arts can easily adapt this method for discussions of historical events such as the 47 ronin, Japan's annexation of Korea, George Silver's attitude problem when it came to Italian fencing, or medieval Europe's ambivalent attitude toward tournaments.

Within the Teaching for Wisdom program, there are three components to these historical discussions. Students are encouraged to think "reflectively, dialogically, and dialectically."

Reflectively: Reflective thinking involves developing an awareness of one's own thought processes. This becomes especially important when we consider the role that values play in wise choices. Far too often, people employ their values in making decisions, but engage in the self-deceptive practice of doing so mindlessly, thus convincing themselves that they are simply doing what any intelligent person would do.

Aside from the arrogance that this mindset engenders, this also renders the person incapable of discussion with someone who does not agree with their ideals. The tendency is to dismiss any opponents as "stupid" or "crazy," without giving thought to the possibility that they might be operating out of their own set of values. I am not arguing for moral relativism here. I am simply putting forward the idea that it is entirely possible for someone to be a sane, intelligent, decent human being, and still disagree with me about important issues. Further, it is also entirely possible to believe that one is correct and that someone else is incorrect, while still acknowledging the opponent as sane, intelligent, and decent. After all, wise people have been arguing about the right thing to do since time immemorial. In fact, reflective thinking can make it easier for one to debate against opponents. Those who are aware of their own values, and have thought them through, will be in a much better position to defend them in a debate, and successfully arguing against an opposing position requires a thorough knowledge of that position. So knowledge of one's own values and the values of others can be a great asset, not only in making wise decisions, but also in the ongoing battle of ideas.

Dialogically: As can be seen in the description of Sternberg's theory, wisdom requires an appreciation of multiple points of view, and of the idea that a problem may have more than one solution. While studying the Boston Massacre, students in the Teaching for Wisdom Program read differing accounts of the event from the American and British sides, leading them toward the idea that an accurate understanding of an event might not be found in a one-sided representation.

Dialectically: We live in a world of paradox. It is considered a maxim of Western political philosophy that liberty is impossible without the rule of law. Existentialists such as Viktor Frankl claim that happiness is only possible after we stop making happiness our goal in life. Christian theologians work toward reconciling descriptions of God as being both a God of holy justice and a God of merciful love. Mahayana Buddhists claim that individual selves both exist and do not exist. Political debates often require that we deal with conflicts between the good of individuals and the good of the group. Atheists strive for a life of purpose while maintaining a belief in the inherent purposelessness of life.[22]

Dialectical thinking involves a willingness to grapple with such paradoxes, and an understanding that, through this process of grappling with opposing principles, ideas have changed and developed across the centuries. This approach to teaching wisdom not only urges students toward a more complex and sophisticated understanding of the world, but also assists them in seeing their areas of study as living fields of inquiry, growing out of the conceptual conflicts of history, embedded within current debates about the legitimacy of rival claims, and moving toward a future continuation of the conversation, to which they may contribute.

While the Teaching for Wisdom Program places a heavy emphasis on encouraging students to integrate the opposing prin-

---

22. Martin Seligman attempts this in his book *Authentic Happiness* (2002, Free Press).

ciples into a synthesis of the two, there are other possibilities for
dealing with the paradoxical nature of seemingly-contradictory
positions.

One possibility is to "pick a side," elevate one of the positions to
the status of being "more right" than the other, and to then attempt
to adequately explain the seeming contradiction in those terms.
To use the previously-mentioned holy/loving God paradox within
Christian theology as an example, theologian Roger Olson claims
that one of the key differences between Calvinist and Arminian
theology is that Calvinists reconcile the holy/loving God paradox
by making God's sovereign holiness the primary attribute, with his
love existing as subordinate attribute that must be understood in
light of God's holiness, while Arminians elevate God's love to primary status and examine his holiness in light of his love. Working
with the political example of handling conflict between collective
and individual interests, libertarians serve as another example of
dealing with paradox by explaining one side in terms of the other.
In this case, the good of the group is defined in terms of the degree
of liberty afforded to the constituent individuals.

Another possibility is to maintain that the two concepts must
be held in a state of dynamic tension, with neither extreme allowed to dominate the other. This idea should be readily comprehensible to students of Asian martial arts, as an obvious example
of this is the dynamic tension existing between the Yin and Yang
principles, as illustrated by the swirling black-and-white *taiji*
symbol. The *taiji* is intended to be a visual representation of the
transformational process of the universal Tao. Yang (the bright,
active, firm, and masculine) coexists with the Yin (the dark, passive, soft, and feminine), but one cannot be reduced to the other.
Neither can one exist without the other, for they are only seen and
understood in their interaction. Trying to understand Yin or Yang
separately would be like trying to understand ballroom dancing
by examining one dance partner while ignoring the other, so an
emphasis solely on motivating students toward a singular synthesis of opposing principles would not always be applicable.

The decision to reconcile opposing concepts either by elevating one or maintaining both can be seen in the ongoing debate within the martial arts regarding the use of forms/kata. On the "pro kata" side of the argument are ideas such as the necessity of maintaining the historical lineage of the traditional forms (Dave Lowry refers to practitioners of traditional martial arts as "living antiques"), their usefulness for teaching core components of the art, or their usefulness as "moving meditation" methods for attaining the proper mindset.

On the "anti kata" side of the argument are the criticism of forms as rigidly artificial (one of the central concepts in Bruce Lee's thought), the psychological disconnect between the cool idealism of kata practice and the chaos and panic of a real-world fight, and the tendency for forms practice to devolve into performance art with much flash but no substance. Criticisms of kata are often put forward by those who argue for greater "realism" in training, and prefer a heavy emphasis on sparring and competition.

The centrality of kata to arts such as Tai Chi Chuan serves as an example of one side of this conflict, focusing on forms training without sparring. The lack of kata in Brazilian Jiu Jitsu can serve as an example of the opposite approach. Other martial arts incorporate both approaches into their training. Shotokan Karate training, for example, centers around the three "k"s: *kihon, kata,* and *kumite* (basic techniques, forms, and sparring), and practitioners maintain that all three must be maintained for complete training. Deciding where one stands on such issues requires the kind of serious thought that is characteristic of a person who is growing in wisdom.

While methods for cultivating wisdom, such as the study of history's great texts and wrestling with the paradoxes of existence, have tremendous value, it is worthwhile to note that these methods are incomplete. Alongside the notion that wisdom may be acquired through intellectual activity, there is the notion that, in many ways, wisdom only comes through experience. Sternberg connects this to the idea of "tacit knowledge," which includes the "unspoken rules" of how to behave in a given situation.

Successfully raising children, for example, may be assisted by listening to the teachings of experts on parenting, but no textbook can completely prepare you to be a parent, or equip you with a systematic technical method for navigating all the excruciatingly complex decisions that must be made in day-to-day life. An operations manual may be a vital component of running a business, but the day-to-day realities of how best to interact with clients and coworkers is something that must be learned in a hands-on context. Similarly, cultivating wisdom among students of the martial arts will require extensive personal experience as well as study. At some level, the best that we can do is to assist people as they work on their own to acquire the necessary experience to be considered wise.

8

Benevolence

The bravest are the tenderest, the loving are the daring.
                                                    Bayard Taylor

Katsujinken, satsujinken.
The sword the gives life,
not the sword that takes life,
is the goal for the Yagyu swordsman.
                                        Yagyu Shinkage Ryu proverb

On February 3rd, 1943, the US Army transport ship *Dorchester* was torpedoed by a German U-Boat. The ship sank within twenty minutes, and of the 902 on board, only 230 survived. Among the dead were four chaplains, one of whom was a Methodist minister (Rev. George L. Fox), one Reformed (Rev. Clark V. Poling), one Roman Catholic (Fr. John P. Washington), and one Jewish (Rabbi Alexander D. Goode). As the ship sank, the four chaplains could be seen busily tending to others' wounds, calming those who were frightened, preaching courage to those struggling, and offering prayers for the dead and dying. One participant in these events, Private William Bednar, claimed that it was only due to their encouragement that he was able to survive amidst the icy waters and hazardous debris. As the people were moved topside, the chaplains took charge of lifejacket distribution. When the lifejackets were all gone, without hesitation they stripped off their own jackets and gave them away. As the ship sank beneath the waves, the four chaplains could be seen, arms linked, praying.

For their selfless actions, all four chaplains were posthumously awarded the Purple Heart and the Distinguished Service Cross. Congress attempted to honor them with the Medal of Honor, but were prevented by a technicality. So a one-time-only Special Medal for Heroism was authorized, and President Eisenhower officially awarded it to them on January 18th, 1961. Congress declared February 3rd, the day the *Dorchester* was torpedoed, "Four Chaplains Day." On February 3rd, 1951, the Four Chaplains Memorial Chapel was dedicated by President Truman. In his dedication speech, the President said: "this interfaith shrine... will stand through long generations to teach Americans that as men can die heroically as brothers, so should they live together in mutual faith and goodwill."[23]

Defining Benevolence

The word "benevolence" comes from two Latin words, meaning "good" and "will." Israeli ethicist and legal scholar Yuval Livnat defines a benevolent act as one that is motivated by a feeling of caring, intending to alleviate the suffering or promote the welfare of the target, and he defines a benevolent person as "a person who tends to care about other human beings, is generally concerned about other people's well-being, and is motivated to perform acts which are aimed at doing good." Some associated concepts that we will be covering in the literature on this topic include "altruism," "compassion," "love," and "care."

---

23. Originally located at Valley Forge, the chapel now stands at the Philadelphia Naval Shipyard, and is dedicated to the mission of promoting cultural and interfaith harmony. The full stories of the chaplains can be found at www.fourchaplains.org, the website of the Four Chaplains Memorial Foundation.

When we bring together the various approaches that scholars have taken to these concepts, they converge on a definition for benevolence. A benevolent person is characterized by a concern for the well-being of others, and a tendency to act in accordance with that concern. If there is a need, the benevolent person takes action to see that the need is met. If there is an opportunity to make someone's life better, the benevolent person takes that opportunity. If there is suffering, the benevolent person strives to alleviate it. Benevolent warriors, then, are those who use their martial skills and abilities out of a motivation to preserve and enhance the well-being of others.

In a previous chapter, we were introduced to the ongoing debate between the "ethic of justice" and the "ethic of care." Due to the work of prominent philosophers such as Immanuel Kant and John Rawls, justice has been the more influential of the two, and Lawrence Kohlberg's justice-based theory of moral development has overwhelmingly dominated the field of moral education.

Recall that, in Kohlberg's theory, individuals who are advancing toward higher levels of morality resolve ethical dilemmas by leaving selfishness behind, growing through a period of concentrating on interpersonal relationships, and then moving on toward the highest stages by making decisions based on abstract principles of universal justice. For Kohlberg, basing decisions on the relationships we have with people we care about indicates a lower level of moral development.

Kohlberg's theory and research were strongly criticized, however, by psychologist Carol Gilligan. In particular, Gilligan was displeased with Kohlberg's finding that women tended to demonstrate systematically "lower" levels of moral reasoning compared to men. Women who participated in Kohlberg's studies tended to make moral decisions based on relational principles of caring more often than on impersonal principles of justice, and Kohlberg interpreted this finding as society holding women back, not allowing them to develop to a man's level. Gilligan argued that this was not an indicator of women's moral retardation, but instead was an indicator of a "different voice" in moral development. This different voice is described as an "ethic of care." Rather than the fairness-based principles of justice, the logic of care operates according to "a psychological logic of relationships." By this relational logic, a moral problem is approached as "one of obligation to exercise care and avoid hurt." The ultimate sin within an ethic of justice is to violate impartiality, treating people unequally, while the ultimate sin within an ethic of care is to act selfishly, treating people hurtfully.

Some people have focused on the fact that research on this approach to ethics often centers around an examination of gender differences, and have described the ethic of care as a uniquely female perspective. This assessment, however, does not concur with Gilligan's research. While she found that female participants tended to speak from the perspective of care more often than the male participants did, Gilligan observed both care and justice operating in both genders, and saw that maturity in moral reasoning for both men and women involved a growing appreciation for the complementary nature of justice and caring, leading Joan Tronto to assert that "an ethic of care is just a set of sensibilities that every morally mature person should develop, alongside the sensibilities of justice morality," and that all people should be encouraged to develop both moralities. According to Gilligan, the morally-advanced person is highly skilled in both ethical systems, able to bring either perspective to bear toward the resolution of problems as the situation calls for it.

As we have seen earlier, Confucian thought has had a tremendous impact on Asian warrior ethics. Philosopher Chenyang Li makes the claim that Confucian ethics can be understood as an ethic of care, adding additional weight to the notion that the ethic of care is not "feminist ethics," and giving this approach greater applicability for our discussion of martial virtues.

Confucian thought on self-cultivation considers the virtue of *jen*[24] to be the supreme characteristic of the advanced person. In the scholarly literature on this topic, *jen* has been translated as "benevolence," "humaneness," "humanity," "love," "compassion," and "charity." While people often tend to get the impression that Confucianism is a rigidly conformist way of life, someone who has a high degree of *jen* understands right action to such an advanced degree that he or she is able to transcend any specific set of rules. Confucian ethics is deeply interpersonal in nature, focusing on family relationships to the degree that political activity is approached as if the nation is an extended family, and the ruler is its father.[25] To act rightly as a Confucian is to fulfill one's role by being a good child, parent, spouse, or citizen, guided by one's natural motivation to care for the members of your family. A Confucian warrior acts to protect his family, and he sees his fellow-countrymen as an extension of that family. Because this tendency to care about family is a basic component of humanity, the more *jen* one manifests, the more fully human one becomes.

Benevolence is also central to Buddhism and Christianity. Buddhist enlightenment eliminates the division between self and other. If there is no real difference between the benefit and suffering of some other person and the benefit and suffering of the self, then the result is a desire to do good to all living beings, and to reduce all beings' suffering. For a Buddhist warrior, this form of benevolence includes reducing people's suffering by defending them.

Within the Christian tradition, work on this topic has typically centered around the term *agape*, and the biblical passage found in the 13th chapter of Paul's first letter to the Corinthians. The word *agape* was coined by the authors of the New Testament to refer to a very specific form of love. Agape is a self-sacrificial form of

---

24. This is sometimes transliterated as "ren."

25. During a debate in Richmond, Virginia during the 1992 U.S. Presidential race, an audience member asked a question in which he described American citizens as "symbolic children" of the President. This comment caused a minor controversy, but would have fit perfectly if the United States were based on Confucian thought rather than Enlightenment social contract theory.

love that equalizes all humanity as members of God's creation, equal recipients of God's love. As God is the source of all value, and all humans are beloved by God, then all humans are given the tremendous value that this love carries with it. As God loves us, so we are to love each other, and Christians see Jesus' sacrifice on the cross as the ultimate expression of God's love. A Christian warrior sacrifices himself by placing his own body in harm's way so that others can live.

The implications of an ethic of care to the life of a warrior may also be found by examining an unlikely pairing of thinkers: feminist ethicist Virginia Held and science fiction author Robert Heinlein. In her book, Held states that an ethic of care is focused on "the compelling moral salience of attending to and meeting the needs of the particular others for whom we take responsibility."

So what needs and what responsibility do we see in the life of a warrior? In his controversial militaristic novel *Starship Troopers,* Heinlein makes a statement that has found a strong resonance among many warriors. When asked what moral characteristic is the distinguishing feature of a soldier, a character (speaking Heinlein's view) replies, "A soldier accepts personal responsibility for the safety of the body politic of which he is a member, defending it, if need be, with his life. The civilian does not." While Heinlein divides his future society into warriors and non-warriors, our situation is more complex, as we can see by the number of people who strive to live in accordance with martial values and traditions (such as students of the martial arts), but are not currently serving as professional protectors in fields such as the military or law enforcement. We may still, however, make use of Heinlein's statement as an indicator of one of the key elements that characterizes a warrior: the acceptance of personal responsibility for the safety of others.

And who are the others? If we hold to an ethic of care, especially if informed by Buddhist compassion and/or Christian agape, the answer must be "everyone." All people are legitimate recipients of a warrior's benevolence. Motivated by concern for their well-being, parents forcefully defend their children, siblings stand side by side when one or the other is threatened, spouses eagerly place themselves in jeopardy for the sake of their partner. Within the context of such intimate family relationships, the connection between benevolent motivation and defensive action is unproblematic. If the circle of care is expanded to encompass neighbors or fellow citizens, many will put their lives on the line in defense of their community or nation.

But what about complete strangers? Who among us are willing to risk their lives in defense of someone with no easy-to-see connection to the self? During the Holocaust, an estimated 50,000 to 500,000 Gentiles (non-Jews) took action to protect persecuted Jews, risking their own lives in defense of other people who were not of their family, not of their religion, not of their ethnicity, and in most cases, not even of their prior acquaintance. This willingness to take personal responsibility for the safety and well-being of strangers took a tremendous amount of courage and compassion, and also fits well with the notion that warriorhood is not necessarily restricted to those who are active in military service.[26]

Political psychologist Kristen Monroe provides one example of this kind of heroism, a German man by the name of Otto, whom she interviewed. Although his status as an ethnic German provided him with considerable benefits under the Nazi regime, his compassion for the persecuted Jews led him to abandon those benefits in favor of serving those to whom he had no prior connection. He was active in the Austrian underground, protected a Jewish woman by marrying her, forged documents, and bribed Gestapo officials and camp guards. Although this resulted in him being sent to a concentration camp himself, he saved over one hundred Jews from imprisonment and slaughter.

---

26. The famous Holocaust rescuer Corrie ten Boom, for example, was a fifty-year-old watchmaker. Despite a complete lack of training in anything resembling warrior skills, she bravely facilitated the escape of several hundred Jews from occupied Holland, and endured the horrors of the Ravensbruck concentration camp.

Monroe examined the motivations for those who risked the lives of themselves and their families to save persecuted Jews, as did Fagin-Jones & Midlarsky. Both sets of researchers found motivational patterns that fit well within an ethic of care and our examination of the virtue of benevolence. Fagin-Jones and Midlarsky's research involved comparing the personalities of rescuers against those of equivalent non-rescuers (these were people, labeled as "bystanders" by the authors, who inhabited areas occupied by Nazi forces during the same time period, but did not engage in any rescue activities). They also compared the situational aspects of these people's lives (marital status, geographic location and living arrangements, personal experience of persecution, etc). Above all other variables, the feature that most strongly distinguished rescuers from bystanders was their belief in the rightness of helping those who are in need, their ability to feel compassion for those who are suffering, and willingness to take risks in expressing that compassion. Monroe's interviews with Holocaust rescuers indicated that the common thread for those who took action in defense of those whom the Nazis hunted was a sense of compassion, derived from the perception of a shared humanity between Gentile and Jew. "Altruists," Monroe writes, "share a view of the world in which all people are one."

Altruistic love for family is common. Altruistic love for strangers is rarer, but evident. At the most extreme end of this line of inquiry, what about enemies? Perceiving all humanity as one means that all humanity is within the moral consideration of an ethic of care. This may lead someone to, on an intellectual level, believe in teachings such as the Buddhist notion of universal oneness or the Christian principle of Jesus' love for his enemies. Living this out, however, is vastly different than agreeing to the principle, and this becomes especially troublesome when applied to warriorhood. Is it possible to love the one you fight? In the case of warfare, or some of the more extreme forms of self-defense, is it possible to love the one you kill?

Some who hold to a love-based ethic say that it is not. Nancey Murphy and George Ellis, for example, argue that a self-sacrificial love is ultimately incompatible with any form of violence or coercion. Even entanglements, such as one might see in Judo or wrestling, are considered by Murphy and Ellis to be painful and coercive, and thus unloving. Only a complete pacifism, they claim, is truly compatible with this kind of morality.

Others disagree. Comte-Sponville, for example, claims that, when taken to this kind of extreme, pacifism takes the virtue of gentleness (a form of benevolence) to such an absolute degree that it nullifies all the other virtues. If perfection in any virtue requires perfection of all the virtues, then no virtue can be permitted to eliminate another. If you see another person in danger (Comte-Sponville uses the example of fighting to save a child's life) you may decide to be benevolent toward the attacker and not violently restrain him. That might work if you are able to nonviolently prevent the intended murder. But a nonviolent benevolence toward the attacker which fails to prevent the murder is a violation of justice, because the child does not deserve to die, and it is also incompatible with benevolence toward the victim.

Virginia Held similarly claims that the ethics of care do not necessarily rule out the use of force when absolutely necessary. On the other hand, while force may be permissible as a last resort, Held says that if we follow the ethics of care, we will be motivated to avoid all hurt, including hurt toward the attacker. Therefore, we must view those who engage even in justifiable forms of violence "as having morally failed to develop appropriate ways to avoid needing to do so," a view with which Shotokan Master Teruyuki Okazaki agrees. Our first priority must be to the prevention of conflict, then to the nonviolent resolution of conflict, then to restraining the aggressor without harming him, and only finally to the violent resolution of conflict.

Aikido master Terry Dobson tells the story of an episode from his younger days that took place on a train in Tokyo. Encountering a violently drunken man who was abusing other railway passengers, Dobson's thoughts immediately turned to the possibility of using his burgeoning martial skills to subdue the aggressor in an act of heroic violence. As he prepared to do so, however, he watched as a little old man gained the aggressive drunk's attention, and began gently talking to him. The kindness of the old man defused the situation, and as Dobson got off the train, the drunken man was quietly weeping in the old man's lap. Dobson felt crude and dirty for having immediately assumed that violence was the only appropriate response to the hostile situation, and this sentiment fits well with Held's and Okazaki's claims that the truly benevolent person exhausts all nonviolent options before falling back on coercion and force.

Okazaki makes the claim that the principle of giving priority to nonviolent solutions to conflict is inherent to Karate. "It isn't accidental," he says, "that, while training, the first move we make from *shizen tai* (ready/natural position) is a block, and that each *kata* begins with a blocking technique." This presumption that the opponent will always be the one to strike first provides opponents with every opportunity to accept our attempts toward nonviolent solutions, and it is a way to demonstrate that we care about our opponents.

Varieties of Benevolence

Mercy

A form of benevolence that is especially relevant to a warrior's life is mercy, which Comte-Sponville defines as a tendency and willingness to forgive an offense. Dispelling some of the misconceptions that may exist about what it means to forgive someone, scholars within the research literature on forgiveness agree on what mercy does *not* require. Mercy is not pretending that the offense never occurred, or that it "wasn't that bad." "Forgiveness is different from pardoning (which is, strictly speaking, a legal concept); condoning (which involves justifying the offense); excusing (which implies that a transgression was committed because of extenuating circumstances); forgetting (which implies that the memory of the transgression has decayed or slipped out of conscious awareness); and denial (which implies an unwillingness or inability to perceive the harmful injuries that one has incurred)."

Philosopher Robert Roberts points to the difference between the emotion of our angry reaction to an offense, and our moral judgment of the perpetrator as guilty of having done something wrong. When we show mercy, forgiving someone for having offended against us, we keep the judgment that the person has done something wrong, and that the offense is neither excusable nor insignificant. What we abandon is our hatred and desire for vengeance. Vengeance is motivated by a desire to make the offender suffer, and to teach the offender a lesson that you are not someone to be trifled with. Revenge is therefore an act of the ego, our basic moral enemy.

But what about the 47 ronin? In the chapter on justice, their vendetta was described as a virtuous act of loyalty. So must we see this as a conflict of virtues, a moral dilemma? Not necessarily. For one thing, the revenge undertaken by the ronin was on behalf of their lord, not of themselves. Roberts makes the point that forgiveness can only be properly applied to offenses committed against yourself. The victim is the one who is in the moral position to either extend or withhold mercy; it cannot be done by a third party. So if, for example, someone were to attack me, I could forgive this person. My brother, however, could not declare the person forgiven for attacking me. If the egocentric nature of revenge is the key element of its vicious nature, then a vendetta undertaken in response to an offense against another person, especially one who does not have the capacity to seek any kind of redress themselves, could be a selfless rather than selfish action.

Another aspect of the situation that demands attention is the fact that the ronin were wiling to face the death penalty as a consequence of their actions. In fact, they turned themselves in to be executed after beheading Kira, indicating that they understood the seriousness of what they did.

Any reader who hopes to use this section of the book as a moral justification for revenge will find less help than they may have hoped. If we are using the 47 ronin as our guide, then the modern analogy would be to exact revenge for an offense committed against someone else (never the self), and then to immediately turn oneself in to the police and offer a full confession, plead guilty, and willingly accept whatever sentence the court hands down. That is the level of self-sacrifice that is required for a morally-justifiable vendetta. So count the cost before determining whether or not the traditional justice system is inadequate to provide a response to an offense.

"Even after a 9, never a 10." Bujinkan Grandmaster Masaaki Hatusmi interprets this Japanese proverb as, among other possibilities, a call for merciful restraint in the fight. "Even in victory," he advises, "do not kill or main an opponent." Settling violent encounters with restraint is another way of demonstrating care for one's opponent.

Okazaki relates a story of Shotokan founder Gichin Funakoshi: "Once I was on a train with him in Japan, and a man pickpocketed him. Master Funakoshi caught his arm, twisted it, and said quietly 'Don't do that again,' That was it." Clearly a martial artist of Funakoshi's caliber was capable of inflicting considerable damage to the thief, damage that might even have been justifiable (one could argue that it would be harder for the thief to pick pockets in the future with broken fingers). The "fat relentless ego" would demand vengeance for daring to violate the pocket of such an important person, but Funakoshi subdued his ego, forgoing vengeance in favor of simply delivering a stern warning. That is mercy. In rare and extreme situations, it may be necessary to kill. But even in these situations, it is possible to demonstrate restraint and mercy by killing as quickly and painlessly as possible.

Compassion

Compassion is another major component of benevolence. It is, in fact, a central motivational feature in the warrior's life. The word "compassion" is derived from the Latin word *pati* (to suffer), with the prefix *cum* (along with). Compassion literally means to "suffer with" someone, and is defined by researchers Susan Sprecher and Beverley Fehr in terms of "caring, concern, tenderness, and an orientation toward supporting, helping, and understanding the other, particularly when the other is perceived to be suffering or in need." A compassionate warrior is one who acts out of a desire to alleviate the suffering of others, or to spare others from the suffering that would result from victimization.

In 1st Corinthians 13, the aforementioned biblical passage on love, we are told that, among other behaviors, love "always protects." A benevolent warrior takes this to heart, and expresses a compassionate love by fighting to remove or prevent threats. In the Thomistic tradition, war is seen as a benevolent act of Christian agape if the purpose of the war is to achieve peace and justice for the people, and is carried out in accordance with that principle.

In medieval Japan, Buddhist compassion informed the self-sacrificial ethic of the samurai class, encouraging them to consider the well-being of others as well worth the risk of their own lives. Dave Lowry considers the self-sacrificial compassion found in the ethic of bushido to be the reason that, when Christianity was introduced to Japan in the sixteenth century, its most profound impact was among Japan's warriors.

Benevolence in Interaction with other Virtues

Benevolence is another that can boast of strong support for the position of supreme virtue. If we focus on the social nature of humanity, and thus the social nature of the virtues, the strength of benevolence's case is clear. After all, if you act with love for another person, you will naturally fulfill all moral requirements as you work for the well-being of that person. Caring about the emotional well-being of another, for example, will result in a drive to maintain one's own emotional self-control, so as to avoid offence.

Desiring the best for another will ensure that you exert all your wisdom in determining exactly what is the best for them.

Examples of those who consider benevolence to be the supreme virtue include psychologist Christopher Peterson, sociologist Pitrim Sorokin, Rabbi Joseph Telushkin, and philosophers Iris Murdoch, Nancey Murphy, and André Comte-Sponville.

On a personal note, if I were to choose among the virtues in this book, and select one as the supreme virtue, benevolence would be my choice. I base this choice on the fundamental premise of my approach to the virtues: they are necessary characteristics that we must develop as correctives, with the "fat relentless ego" as the fundamental moral enemy. If the basic form of vice is self-centeredness, then the basic form of virtue is the ability and tendency to focus on others rather than the self. Benevolence, with its emphasis on altruism and self-sacrifice, is the most other-centered of the virtues, making it the one that most directly dislodges the self from the center of our psychological universe.

Whether or not benevolence can be placed at the peak of a virtuous hierarchy, love of others motivates and directs the other virtues. It also requires the other virtues for its truest functioning. Georgetown University Philosopher Alisa Carse points out the morally-problematic nature of misguided compassion. The feeling of "suffering with" someone who is in distress can become unbalanced, resulting in actions that may be motivated by care, but end up being contrary to the well-being of the person in question. One example that she presents involves a parent whose child expresses an earnest desire for fudge. A little parental indulgence every now and then may be okay, but immersing oneself too deeply in the child's (admittedly mild) suffering from the unmet demands of a sweet tooth would result in a never-ending provision of fudge, to the detriment of the child's health.

Compassion requires moderation, bringing the virtue of temperance into play. Carse uses the terms "incuriosity" and "self-effacement" to refer to the intemperate extremes that undermine genuine benevolence. Incuriosity is simply a lack of interest in trying to see things from the other person's perspective, in which case compassion is impossible. Self-effacement is becoming so deeply immersed in the other person's perspective that one loses the ability to see situations from any perspective *but* the other person's. Carse says that we need a "morally contoured empathy," in which feelings of compassion are guided by the ability to look at moral decisions from multiple perspectives. Recalling that practical wisdom involves the ability to use multiple viewpoints to recognize what the relevant aspects of a situation are, benevolence must combine with wisdom as well as temperance in Carse's approach to compassion.

Benevolence combines with temperance to provide a necessary balance in our loving acts. In Comte-Sponville's example of fighting to save a child's life, he balances benevolence toward the attacker against benevolence toward the child. To adopt a extreme pacifist stance, allowing the child to be murdered in the name of caring about the attacker, is to sacrifice one benevolence to another. Our natural inclination, guided by righteous anger over the injustice of a child's murder, is more likely to be toward the opposite extreme of uncontrolled aggression toward the attacker.

This is understandable, and very few people would hold it against you if your anger got the better of you in this kind of situation. To hold up the highest possible standards of virtue, however, the emotional self-mastery provided by the cultivation of temperance would act to restrain our aggression. The goal in a situation like this would be to save the child's life through the use of as little violence as possible.

Virginia Held argues that, in situations like this, those who live by an ethic of care "seek to move toward peace. Practices of care may need to include the use of coercion to restrain a person who is or is threatening to become violent, but the objective is to do so without damaging the person physically or psychologically." Further, Held argues, our responsibility for restraining ourselves increases as our power increases.

Following this logic, advancement in the martial arts, which is characterized by an increasing ability to inflict pain and damage on an opponent, should also be characterized by a corresponding decrease in desire to inflict pain and damage on a opponent. As one becomes more lethal, one must become more gentle, and the combination of benevolence and temperance is vital to this form of growth.

Benevolence and courage are so intertwined that the willingness to face danger and death for the sake of the loved one is considered the ultimate proof and expression of love. Without courage, compassion is not translated into action. While researchers such as Monroe and Oliner focused on the role of compassion and altruistic beliefs in the lives of Holocaust rescuers, Fagin-Jones & Midlarsky found that it was a combination of altruism and courage that distinguished rescuers from bystanders. Others who witnessed the Nazis' persecution of Jews may have felt emotionally moved by their suffering, but the risks involved were too great. Whether this is a case of insufficient compassion, or a case of compassion without sufficient courage, the desire to see an end to the suffering of others was not translated into action. As it is with the other virtues, benevolence without courage is impotent and useless.

The connection between wisdom and benevolence is especially strong in the Buddhist tradition. The Shaolin Ch'an monks, for example, teach four virtues (wisdom, compassion, mercy, kindness) that can be conceptually collapsed into wisdom and benevolence. Other treatments of Buddhist ethics demonstrate variations on this same dual-virtue approach. Conze and Habito claim that wisdom is the highest virtue, with compassion as its outworking. Asvagosha described benevolent action as a means of detaching from the self, thus attaining wisdom. The underlying message is that seeing the world as it really is (that life is suffering, and that no separation exists between self and other), and desiring to ease the suffering of the world's inhabitants, are mutually-supportive activities. The more one sees the world as it really is, the greater the tendency to act with compassion. The more one acts with compassion, the more one's ego is dethroned by the act of helping another. The less egocentric one becomes, the more one comes to see the world as it really is.

As we have seen, the interaction between benevolence and justice is a troublesome one. It is worth noting that the debate between benevolence and justice would not be so contentious if both virtues were not so necessary. If one of these could be dispensed with, the debate would cease. But none of us are prepared to endorse justice without mercy, and one need only look at over-indulgent parents (and the resulting spoiled brats) to see examples of the destructive nature of unjust compassion.

Cultivating Benevolence in Yourself

The work of social psychologist C. Daniel Batson provides the major psychological research from which we can draw an approach to cultivating benevolence. Batson's research has centered around what he called the *empathy-altruism hypothesis*, the proposition that increasing empathy results in increases in motivation to help.

Alisa Carse defines empathy as "the ability and disposition to imagine (as best we can) how others feel, what they fear or hope for, and how they understand themselves and their circumstances." Empathy involves viewing situations from another person's perspective, and empathy research has demonstrated that imagining oneself in another person's place results in a reduced desire to harm others, more pro-social/moral behavior in general, and increases in helping behavior. By practicing empathy, then, we can develop greater benevolence.

When psychologists experimentally study empathy, research participants are typically presented with a situation, and are instructed to try to imagine how the person in the situation feels, and how the situation affects that person's life.

Azy Barak, a psychology professor at the University of Haifa, put this method to use in a "game" designed to increase the empathy of counselors-in-training, a game which may be adapted by those who wish to cultivate empathy, and thus benevolence, in themselves. Barak's empathy game involves evaluating written statements by hypothetical counseling clients. In the statements, the clients describe various life situations (estranged daughter, extramarital affair, feelings of worthlessness, etc.). The trainees are given these statements and are asked to imagine the thoughts, desires, emotions, and so on, that are behind the statements.

Martial artists who wish to make use of this procedure in making themselves more empathic might try this technique while reading books or news items. Don't just skip over the story in the newspaper about an abusive parent being arrested, or about the funeral announcement for an elderly person. Slow down for a minute to think about it. Think about the story from the perspective of those involved, and ask yourself how that person might feel, and how it would affect that person's life, and how you would feel if it happened to you. What do you think it might feel like, for example, to lose someone to whom you have been married for fifty years? Half a century, and now that person is just not there anymore. If the story involves any first-person narratives (Barak's hypothetical statements were written in first person), place special focus on those statements.

Johanna Shapiro trains medical students at the University of California-Irvine. Emphasizing the importance of empathy in physicians, she also focuses on the role that stories play in its cultivation. Using an elective course on literature and medicine, Shapiro and her colleagues engaged a group of medical students in reading and discussing short stories, poetry, and skits. These bits of literature all touched on topics that relate to medicine, and were intended to enhance empathy and compassion in the reader (pain, sexuality, lifestyle adjustments, examinations, etc.). Reading and discussing these stories resulted in measurable increases in the students' ability to empathize.

Movies can serve a similar function. Although films typically present us with sanitized and simplified visions of reality, we may nevertheless carry away some of the sympathy and compassion portrayed by the characters.

Martial artists, by and large, love martial arts movies. Yes, we know that they're often cheesy. Yes, the acting is usually awful. Yes, the plot is typically a flimsy excuse to string together the fight scenes. And yes, most of the characters rarely rise to the level of two-dimensionality (three dimensions is usually too much to hope for). But the demonstrations of skill and athleticism by the actors and stunt performers are delights to the eye. How many of us in the martial arts community were inspired to start training by a Chuck Norris kick, or Bruce Lee's lighting-fast hands? The inspiring effect of the movies is itself a statement of their motivational value.

Can these films teach us benevolence? It depends on the film. A typical martial arts film usually involves either a motivation toward justice or toward benevolence on the part of the hero, but too often this is presented fleetingly so as not to distract from the fighting, and some films are straightforward tales of egocentric revenge. Some movies, however, do place a heavier emphasis on the martial artist as a person of compassion.

One of my favorites, for example, is the 1989 film *Best of the Best.* Eric Roberts' histrionic facial contortions notwithstanding, I consider it to be a fairly well-made martial arts movie (and who doesn't like James Earl Jones?) that provides a slightly different perspective on the vendetta by providing the character Tommy with a moral victory through an act of mercy. It is an act that results in the forging of a relationship with the "villain" of the film (which proves to be useful in *Best of the Best II*).

Another aspect of the film, one that ties in to my next point about cultivating benevolence, is in the treatment of the Korean competitors. As the villains of the film, the members of the Korean team are presented, as such villains often are, as relatively impersonal fighting machines. However, after the competition, the "villains" are revealed to be every bit as human as the American team, demonstrating integrity, remorse, and amiability. When that happened, the Koreans were shown to be very similar to their American counterparts, and they shifted from being "Them" to being "Us."

The concept of moral inclusion involves the principle of widening our perception of which groups of people are legitimate recipients of our benevolence. As we previously discussed, at its highest level the ethic of care is extended to all beings, and the Holocaust rescuers clearly demonstrated this widened range of compassion. By learning compassion for those whom we would not previously consider worthy of our love, we develop into better human beings.

Batson talks about widening the "scope of empathy" in terms of "adopting" people into our range of caring. This concept parallels the method of developing benevolence found in the thought of Meng Tzu (Mencius), the fourth-century BCE Confucian scholar. Mencius, like other Confucians, considered *jen* (benevolence) to be the supreme virtue, and described the cultivation of *jen* to be a matter of examining our responses to certain situations, and then extending those reactions to new situations.

Nobody, Mencius would argue, could help but feel compassion and an urgent motivation to help if they saw a small child about to fall down a well. Cultivating benevolence can take the form of recognizing similarities between these clear-cut situations and the various situations that we encounter in our lives. Extending compassion to a stranger, for example, may involve recognizing that this person is somebody's son/daughter, somebody's brother/sister, and so on. How would I feel, and what would I do, if it was *my* brother in distress? The answer to that question answers the question of how I should react when I see a stranger in distress. Practicing thinking in these terms goes a long way toward becoming a more benevolent person.

Several scholars have connected Buddhist meditation practices to this kind of expansion of our range of compassion. In the "loving kindness" meditative practice, the one who is meditating repeats the phrases: "May I be free from suffering. May I find my joy. May I be filled with love. May I be at peace." Genuinely wishing for this is not difficult, as it is our natural inclination to wish the best for ourselves. Next, these phrases are repeated, but with the "I" replaced with the name of a someone who has recently done something good for you. This is one step away from the self, but still an easy wish to make. As the method progresses, the targets of the meditation get further and further removed from the self. You wish happiness and love to a close friend, then to a stranger, then to someone with whom you recently had a conflict, then to an enemy, and finally to all humanity. If done properly, the benevolence that one naturally feels toward oneself is gradually extended to more and more difficult recipients.

Christians who wish to explore similar concepts might do so by following Jesus' instructions regarding praying for one's enemies (Matthew 6:44). The prayer could begin by asking God's blessings on friends and family members, and moving toward prayers for strangers and for enemies, in a manner similar to the Buddhist loving kindness practice.

Rabbi Telushkin encourages his readers to practice a form of selective interpretation as a way of cultivating empathy in our judgments of other people's actions. When we do something that might be inconvenient or rude to another person, we tend to rationalize it by focusing on our good intentions or mitigating circumstances. Afford other people the same consideration. If someone's behavior could be interpreted in more than one way, choose the interpretation that produces the more favorable judgment of that person. Don't assume that you know the person's evil heart when he does something wrong. This does not mean abandoning justice. We are to exercise sound judgment both when evaluating our own actions and when evaluating the actions of others. However, people have a tendency to cut themselves too much slack, and other people not enough slack. Counteract this tendency by judging yourself more harshly, and other people more mercifully.

In practically living out our attempts to develop greater levels of benevolence, a natural place for us to begin is in the training hall. When discussing contract-based approaches to justice, I previously mentioned that the martial arts must maintain the belief that training is not "all about me." We are here for each other. Fulfilling our roles in a practice setting is one manifestation of that.

At a more emotional level, cultivating benevolence should include the development of a deep caring for students, and for the instructor. As an everyday example, I have very often seen two students engaged in practice drills, and one student will knock the other off his or her feet. Immediately, the knock-er will ask "Are you all right?", and offer a hand up to the other student. Some people refuse the helping hand up, perhaps seeing it as a sign of weakness. However, in reality the offer is usually a sign of caring. If you are not already in the habit of displaying concern for the well-being of your fellow students, begin to establish that habit as one more step toward becoming a more benevolent person.

Cultivating Benevolence in Others

The methods discussed earlier for the cultivation of empathy through the reading and discussion of stories were developed primarily for the fostering of empathy in others, and are only secondarily being adapted here for solo use. Rather than meditating alone on the emotions behind a character's actions or reactions, those who wish to assist others in developing benevolence may engage them in discussions of how other people feel in certain situations.

Specifically, Azy Barak focuses on four questions that we are to ask about the hypothetical statements in his "empathy game": (1) What is the person saying about themselves? (2) What emotions are being communicated in the statement? (3) What does the character think is the cause of the problem? (4) What does the character think is the solution?

Discussions on these kinds of topics can be tailored to fit various groups. Martial arts instructors who work with young students might develop some hypothetical stories for group discussion that are relevant to children's lives. To prevent young would-be warriors from becoming young bullies, a discussion may involve requiring students to see from the perspective of a victim of bullying. To teach restraint when confronting injustice ("Even after a 9, never a 10"), the same situation could be examined from the bully's perspective. In this way, nonviolent methods to resolve a confrontation may be explored.

Those who work with adults or older youths may encounter resistance to this approach, as it may strike many as touchy-feely malarkey ("I came here to learn how to boot some head, not to sit through a sensitivity course. What's next, we join hands and sing kumbayah?"). Progress might be made in overcoming students' resistance by introducing the topic in terms of the tactical advantage of seeing through the eyes of an opponent. If one can learn to see from their perspective, one can know their goals, their patterns of interpretation, and their motivations. Know these things, and there is a better chance of predicting what the opponent will do.

Conclusion

Supreme virtue or not, benevolence is vital to the defeat of the ego. Whatever images of a warrior's callous insensitivity we may see in the media, one who wishes to rise above the level of a brute and toward the level of a warrior should adopt "*bushi no nasaké*—the tenderness of the warrior" as a guiding principle. As our power increases, the number of people for whom we take responsibility increases, and so too the amount of care that we must demonstrate increases.

9

Courtesy
(Not a Virtue, but Still Vital)

This is the final test of a gentleman: his respect
for those who can be of no possible value to him.
William Lyon Phelps

A warrior's best weapon is good manners.
Bud Malmstrom

Alexander the Great stands as one of the more controversial figures in history, with portrayals of his character ranging from enlightened visionary to megalomaniacal tyrant. Whether the true motivations behind his actions in the mid 4th century BCE were a generous example of chivalry or a scheming example of Machiavellianism, his reputation in history has been greatly enhanced by his courteous treatment of a certain group of captives.

In 333 BCE, the 23-year-old Alexander had been commander of the League of Corinth for the previous three years. Having put down the Theban rebellion of 335, Greece had been sufficiently secured for Alexander to turn his attention to the Persian Empire, which was under the rule of Darius III. In a battle just south of the town of Issus, Darius' army was routed by Alexander's forces. Darius fled, leaving behind his mother, his wife, and his children. The victorious Alexander promised to treat these royal captives with the courtesy due their station, and they remained well-treated "guests" of his for two years. Alexander's handling of his enemy's family was so gentlemanly that, when Alexander died eight years later, Darius' mother wept for him (some versions of the story describe her as so distraught that she starved herself to death out of grief). In addition to creating a favorable impression on Darius' mother, Alexander's actions created a favorable impression in many biographers. In medieval chivalric literature, Alexander the Great was listed among the Nine Worthies, warriors from history and legend who were held up as examples of virtuous character.

Scholars disagree about whether courtesy or politeness may be properly considered virtues in themselves, or if they should be treated as varieties of higher-order virtues such as justice or benevolence. Moral philosopher Sarah Buss argues that courtesy is itself a virtue. The basis of her argument is humanity's social nature. As we are social beings, we depend on each other and we always act in interaction with each other, so the ability to make other people happy is essential to our functioning. Therefore, Buss claims, we have a "basic moral obligation to make ourselves agreeable to others," and courtesy is the virtue that enables us to fulfill that obligation.

Along similar lines, virtue ethicist Karen Stohr uses goal-oriented logic in her argument that "good manners" is a virtue. As we saw in Chapter Two, in such an approach virtues are understood as characteristics that help us to move toward the lower-level goals of a practice, and the higher-level goals of a human life. Because the ability to behave "appropriately" in social settings enables a person to better pursue excellence and success, Stohr considers courtesy to be the virtue that serves as "the vehicle through which moral commitments are expressed and moral ends are accomplished."

These approaches to courtesy reflect the same ideas found in earlier classics on the subject, such as Giovanni Della Casa's 16th-century book *Galateo*. Della Casa claims that courtesy is the virtue that enables people to navigate their way through civilized life. Courtesy may be a less impressive virtue than justice or courage, but it is more often used in everyday life.

Others (including myself) disagree with this classification, and argue that courtesy is not a virtue in and of itself. André Comte-Sponville claims that politeness is not a virtue, and even if it might be classified as such, it ranks as "the poorest, the most superficial, and the most debatable of the virtues."

Courtesy is a highly valuable characteristic to cultivate, and can be a component of virtuous action, but it is not itself a virtue. Politeness, argues Comte-Sponville, presents the *appearance* of virtuousness, and the polite person treats others with the *appearance* of respect and consideration. It is this artificiality that Comte-Sponville finds suspicious. It is entirely possible, he argues, to be a polite and well-mannered person without having true respect or consideration at all. In fact, a combination of superficial refinement with a cruel heart is more inhuman than barbarism without any pretense of civility.

While I agree with Comte-Sponville's claim that politeness is not a virtue, I disagree with his idea that politeness is nothing but outward show. There is a long tradition in the literature on courtesy, emphasizing that politeness is not really about the specific rules and traditions of table settings and salutations, but is in fact an outward expression of inward virtue.

A 16th-century English courtesy manual *"Institucion of a Gentleman,"* for example, distinguishes between four different kinds of people. The anonymous author makes the distinction between the gentleness of a person's social status and the gentleness of their character. There are the "gentle gentle," those who have high social status and honorable character. There are also the "gentle ungentle," those who have high status but dishonorable character. There are the "ungentle gentle," those who are of low social status, but honorable character. And finally there are the "ungentle un-gentle," those who are of both low status and dishonorable character. Only the "gentle gentle" and the "ungentle gentle" are truly worthy of the title of "gentleman."

Etiquette legend Emily Post refers to a person's manner as "the outward manifestation of one's innate character and attitude towards life," and she considers etiquette to be a form of applied ethics. Stohr agrees that "it's hard to see the proper placement of an oyster fork as a moral issue," but argues that such specifics are not really the point of manners, and that those who hold to the rules of decorum without good character are not truly well-mannered.

This is not to say that the outward and socially-strategic forms of etiquette are irrelevant. Politeness is frequently commended as a method for developing social influence, achieving worldly success, and social climbing. A polite response can be a powerful tool in achieving goals and avoiding problems.

Several people, for example, who run martial arts academies tell stories of "dojo stormers" who arrive uninvited to demand a fight with the head instructor. This practice does have historical roots in the martial arts, and it can conjure up images of honorable combat between masters who wish to test their skill and settle questions of the applicability of their teachings. Unfortunately, this is typically not what happens. The challenger is most often a half-trained loudmouth with too much testosterone and too little brains, and the challenge is nothing more than an annoying disruption. At such times, many instructors have found that politely discussing the challenge and attempting to establish ground rules (such as signing legal waivers, waiting until after the class for the match, or asking what the challenger is willing to put up as a wager on the outcome) is sufficient to take the wind out of the challenger's sails. Thus courtesy becomes a way to eliminate an irritant without having sunk to that person's level.

The fact that politeness is praised for its effectiveness as much as for its excellence could be thought of as one more example of the tension in Western thought between the honorable and the honored. As we have previously seen, the notion of proper behavior has struggled with the discrepancy between the ideal and the actual that is frequently seen when it comes to matters of honor. Ideally, behaving an a manner that is right and proper will both conform to one's high moral character and also be recognized by society as deserving of praise and reward. However, we do not live in an ideal world, and what society honors is not always that which is truly honorable. Mason's literary analysis shows that the idea of proper behavior (rather than high birth) conferring nobility is found in numerous medieval texts. However, medieval courts were in reality shamelessly elitist.

On the other hand, another way of looking at this tension might involve the distinction made by MacIntyre between the "qualities of excellence" and the "qualities of effectiveness," which we discussed back in the first chapter. While the qualities of effectiveness help in the achievement of the external goods of a practice (money, fame, etc.), the qualities of excellence help with achieving the internal goods of a practice, enabling one to be a *good* practitioner. The qualities of effectiveness are necessary for the good person as well as the successful person, and the good person may often be successful. Within the martial arts, examples of the qualities of effectiveness can include strength and skill. Politeness might be considered another of these "overlaps," a form of behavior that both enables external success and assists in the cultivation of excellence.

Dave Lowry discusses politeness as a quality of effectiveness in the martial arts. In addition to being connected to cultivating virtue, etiquette has practical and tactical advantages. In a dangerous world, the fewer people we antagonize, the safer we are. This is especially important in societies in which dueling and/or an armed citizenry is common, and the ability to move and operate in such a society without creating enemies has great usefulness. Looking at it from the opposite perspective, warriors can be frightening people at times. In order to move and operate in society, the ability to make others feel at ease can be useful.

Courtesy while fighting can also have tactical advantages, as showing politeness requires self-control. By developing the ability to follow the rules of etiquette in all circumstances, even in a fight, the result is a calm and controlled self-presentation. You reveal nothing to your opponent. An opponent whose overall behavioral style is exactly the same while fighting as it is during everyday activities is an opponent who is very difficult to read. Cultivate courtesy, and you deprive your enemy of a potential advantage.

It is my argument that, rather than being a virtue itself, courtesy is a way of behaving in which the virtues can be exercised and strengthened. One point in support of this argument is that, when Buss and Stohr describe politeness as a virtue, both support their claims that it is a virtue by pointing to courtesy's ability to embody other virtues. Buss claims that the essential point of good manners is to treat people with the respect to which they are due. When we treat people politely, we acknowledge their inherent dignity. Thus, Buss' treatment of courtesy shows it to be a way of demonstrating justice. Stohr describes good manners as knowledge of how to behave properly in social settings so that you can achieve your moral goals. Knowing the appropriate ways toward moral goals fits Sternberg's balance theory of wisdom and Wink & Nelson's description of a practically wise person as someone who has good interpersonal skills and superior decision-making ability. Stohr's treatment of courtesy shows it to be a way of demonstrating wisdom. So even those who support courtesy's status as a virtue fall back on other virtues in their arguments.

These connections between politeness and other virtues are central to my point about politeness. I believe that courtesy's primary function in a person of good character is practicing and developing the virtues in everyday situations. A single push-up is not a tremendous act of physical strength, and a single "thank you" is not a tremendous act of moral strength. But every small exercise of strength (physical or moral) makes us one small step stronger. Therefore, just as everyday exercise is vital for the physical development of a martial artist, everyday exercise is vital for the martial artist's character development. Politeness is a way to engage in this everyday exercise.

John Ruth considers a polite person to be a person of courage, bold in his opinions, but gentle in the expression of them. As described earlier, social courage involves acting on behalf of what is right in the face of possible mockery or rejection. A coward remains silent when his friends or beliefs are attacked, allowing fear to permit the existence of a verbal injustice. Courtesy provides a way to courageously express oneself and verbally defend others without perpetrating injustice or verbal cruelty toward the other person in the conversation. Courteous behavior involves maintaining one's calm. This equanimity, especially when confronted with rudeness or provocation, conforms to Nitobe's description of "statical" courage. Rude treatment is a threat to the ego, and the fear of being disrespected can be very strong. Calmly ignoring disrespect, or calmly responding to it, is an act of courage, and this feature makes polite behavior an opportunity to practice courage.

Buss, although she claims that courtesy is a virtue on its own, bases her claim on courtesy's capacity for the expression and development of justice. In her treatment of courtesy, she claims that the central function of courteous behavior is to express respect for others. When one expresses respect, others are treated in a way that acknowledges their inherent dignity. Insults and disrespectful behaviors are expressions of injustice, because they treat others as though they possess less value than they really do. Courtesy is a useful method for cultivating interpersonal justice. Buss puts it well:

> To learn that human beings are the sort of animal to whom one must say "please," "thank you," "excuse me," and "good morning," that one ought not to interrupt them when they are speaking, that one ought not to avoid eye contact and yet ought not to stare, that one ought not to crowd them and yet ought not be standoffish, to learn all this and much more is to learn that human beings deserve to be treated with respect, that they are respectworthy, that is, that they have a dignity not shared by those whom one does not bother to treat with such deference and care.

One virtue that is very often associated with courtesy is temperance, and temperance's sub-virtues humility and emotional self-control. While her primary emphasis is on justice, Buss also examines polite behavior as a way of restraining expressions of pride. Humility is demonstrated when one treats others with respect, showing them "that one does not care overly much for one's own dear self."

While some (such as Comte-Sponville) reject the artificial nature of politeness, Stohr embraces it. If politeness sometimes involves acting in ways that we do not feel (we may not feel respectful toward a stupid person, but it is still necessary to express respect in our treatment of that person), that is not an endorsement of insincerity. Instead, it is a humbly honest self-assessment: "etiquette recognizes that, morally speaking, we are not always up to par, and its aim is to prevent us from letting our behavior slide down to the level of our moods." Polite behavior is a way to act virtuously when we do not feel very virtuous, and a recognition that this is necessary is a way of cultivating and expressing humility.

The connection between courtesy and self-control runs through the literature on the subject. John Ruth describes a courteous person as one who puts forward a modest and subdued emotional expression, and Lillian Eichler defines etiquette as "the art of being able to hold oneself always in hand, no matter how exacting the circumstances." In keeping with the notion that temperance involves seeking a healthy moderation between excess and deficiency, politeness does not require that we be closemouthed or unemotional, only that we stay in control of ourselves. Happiness is appropriate under the right circumstances; uncontrolled obnoxious laughter is inappropriate. Anger is appropriate under the right circumstances; outbursts of temper are inappropriate. The courteous person is able to know the right circumstances and the right degree of emotional expressiveness.

The knowledge of when to express one's emotions, and to what degree those emotions should be expressed, is another of the connections between courtesy and wisdom. Blaine Fowers' description of practical wisdom involves the ability to accurately see the important features of a situation, to decide what goals are desirable in the situation, and to know how best to accomplish those goals. Acting politely is exercise in practical wisdom, because a polite person must not only decide how to accomplish goals, but how to do so without creating offense. The wise person also considers courtesy as a tool in the pursuit of goals. Ruth, in considering this strategic aspect of courtesy, states that it is impossible to accomplish our "great designs" unless we are "eminent and respectable before our fellow-beings," and Stohr points out the necessity of a virtuous person being skilled at effectively employing the rules of social interaction toward just goals. Courtesy is both a form of wisdom, and a tool in the hands of wisdom.

Benevolence is the virtue most commonly associated with courtesy. In line with this chapter's message, that courtesy is a way to develop and practice the virtues in everyday situations, John Young says that "politeness is benevolence in small things," an assessment echoed by Inazo Nitobe. Similarly, concern for others is the common theme running through Della Casa's classic work on courtesy, and Ruth states that the polite person always desires "never to wound the feelings of another." This concern for the feelings of others will cover over any flaws in your formal knowledge of etiquette. "Better a generous oaf," Comte-Sponville says, "than a polite egoist, an honorable lout than a refined scoundrel."

Those who do have formal knowledge of etiquette should remember to demonstrate politeness to those who do not have this knowledge. This is sometimes encountered in martial arts circles, especially within some of the more traditional arts in which etiquette plays a large role. Among certain practitioners of *Kenjutsu* (Japanese sword fighting), for example, improper placement of the thumb on the *tsuba* (hand guard) of a sheathed sword could be considered a threat (the level of provocation may be considered similar to a Western gunslinger unsnapping his holster's restraining strap). This detail of sword etiquette is easy for the untrained eye to miss, and not everybody who picks up a katana knows this rule.

More commonly, many training halls require that practitioners bow when entering the training area. What is the courteous response when encountering someone who has their thumb placed in a threatening position, or who does not know when to bow? If you wish to avoid hurting the feelings of the other person, quietly pointing out his error might be preferable to publicly embarrassing him, and it is often easy to discern whether the impolite action is due to an honest mistake or deliberate disrespect.

One of the fundamental principles of Karate is that it begins with a bow and ends with a bow. This fact, says Okazaki, provides a nonverbal embodiment of Karate's system of character development, and sets a tone of respect for the entire encounter between individuals. Okazaki laments the large number of Karate practitioners who are so focused on winning matches in tournaments that their bows become nothing but empty formalities, lacking necessary respect and humility. He warns students that "if you do not show courtesy, you are not a true martial artist."

Even if courtesy is not formally listed as a virtue in this treatment of the warrior virtues, it remains worthy of our attention. From East to West, from bushido to chivalry, a warrior of excellence is expected to be a polite person. In addition to the strategic and social advantages gained by the development of politeness, it is an easily understandable and accessible method for self-cultivation.

Scholars such as Stohr recommend that those who wish to develop politeness in themselves begin with a good book on etiquette. Students of the martial arts may wish to begin with a survey of the rules of etiquette connected with their art. Whether the topic is bows, salutations, ritual phrases, or the handling of weapons, these rules did not spring full-grown out of nowhere. Students would do well to investigate what kind of message is being communicated. By remaining aware of what they are "saying" by these actions in the training hall, students might begin to take steps toward becoming a person of courtesy, and thus a person of greater virtue.

10
Tying It All Together: What's Your Story?

The Sword is the Mind. When the Mind is right, the Sword is right. When the Mind is not right, the Sword is not right. He who would study the Way of the Sword must first study his Mind.

Dennis Schmidt

Studying the martial arts is not something one 'adapts' to his life, but rather one adapts the life to the art. It means changing one's values, attitudes, and behavior. It does not mean taking up a hobby.

Randy Nelson

The Aristotelian approach is teleological. What this means is that, whatever the topic is that is being examined, we have to focus on the *telos*, the goal or purpose of the thing. So then, what is the goal? Why talk about the warrior virtues? Why study the martial arts? If you see the martial arts only as something fun to do with your time, with no more impact on your personality than bowling or attending Star Trek conventions, then reading this book may have been a waste of your time. For those who take the martial arts seriously, however, there is a question that has to be answered: What is the place of the martial arts in your life? The answer to this question is also the answer to the question of the purpose of the warrior virtues.

This examination of the martial virtues has involved defining the martial arts using Alasdair MacIntyre's concept of a "practice." MacIntyre makes the distinction between the external goods of a practice (those benefits that could be obtained through some other activity) and the internal goods of a practice (the specific benefits that can only be had by engaging in the practice), and he points to the idea that the internal goods are the heart of a practice. Dave Lowry's description of what attracts students to traditional martial arts is in line with this understanding of a practice. There is something about these arts that promises a certain kind of life, and the novice wants that kind of life.

Lawrence Kohlberg criticized virtue ethics as nothing more than an offering of a jumbled bag of socially-desirable traits. Without the unifying concept of the kind of life produced by entering into a practice, Kohlberg would be correct. The virtues make sense when understood to be character traits that empower the practitioner's achievement of the internal goods of the practice, equipping the practitioner for living a certain kind of life.

So what kind of unity does a practice, such as the martial arts, provide to the practitioner? By focusing on the pursuit of perfection when performing the practice, MacIntyre describes the unity of a human life in terms of a quest. Given the strong literary connection between warriors and quests, this approach should find strong resonance among students of the martial arts. Within the context of a practice, the virtues help the student's advancement in the martial arts, and within the overall context of a human life, the practice of the martial arts helps one along life's quest.

All quests have goals. In literature, quests involve goals such as the rescue of a captive, the slaying of a monster, or the acquisition of a treasure (a classic example being King Arthur's quest for the Holy Grail). What makes a quest different from other activities, however, is that the goal itself is actually of secondary importance. What is really important is the process of seeking the goal. By pursuing the goal, the hero of a quest grows and advances by facing and overcoming the many obstacles encountered. Maurice Keen points out that the quest for the Holy Grail in Arthurian literature "is not just for the Grail, as an object, but for what it symbolizes: Eucharistic grace and communion in ecstasy with God." In feudal Japan, warriors might engage in the practice of *musha shugyo*, a warrior's quest that involved traveling in search of new opportunities to train and serve.

One of my favorite quest stories is Tolkien's *The Hobbit*. While reading this book, it may occur to some readers that there must have been an easier way to obtain the dragon's treasure (the goal of the quest). The characters do have Gandalf, for instance. Gandalf is a powerful wizard, though one with an inconvenient habit of disappearing for extended periods of time. If Gandalf is as powerful as he is supposed to be, why couldn't he have killed the dragon? Or teleported the gold out from under it? Easier, maybe, but such an approach would have missed the point of the story.

The main characters (especially Bilbo) become very different people by traveling to the dragon's mountain, and that was the real point of *The Hobbit*. This personal transformation would have been impossible if Gandalf had simply appeared at Bilbo's door and said "Hello. You don't know me, but I just transformed a dragon into a bunny rabbit, and I'm giving you one-fourteenth of his treasure, along with this very warm rabbit-fur hat." Bilbo had to endure the quest to learn what he was capable of, and to develop those capabilities. Thorin, leader of the Dwarves, gained a very different education through participating in the quest. Though it cost him his life, Thorin was finally able to see the pointlessness of valuing the treasure above friendship and honorable behavior.

MacIntyre points out that "a quest is not at all the search for something adequately characterized, as miners search for gold or geologists for oil. It is in the course of the quest and only through encountering and coping with the various particular harms, dangers, temptations, and distractions which provide any quest with its episodes and incidents that the goal of the quest is finally to be understood. A quest is always an education both as to the character of that which is sought and in self-knowledge."

This is all well and good for hobbits and King Arthur, but what about real life? Can life be seen as an extended *musha shugyo*? The connection may be stronger than you think. Many scholars are beginning to find themselves in agreement with MacIntyre's claim that life is a narrative quest.

Psychologist Dan McAdams has been developing a "psychology of life stories" based on the idea that people's identities are constructed as personal stories. We tell these stories to each other and to ourselves, and it is in the context of these stories that we come to understand what our lives have been about, what we're currently doing, and where we're trying to go. Life stories bring the scattered elements of a person's life into a somewhat integrated whole, and different kinds of stories will produce different kinds of people. These stories may be simplistic or complex, optimistic or pessimistic, healthy or unhealthy. Based on this kind of theoretical work, psychologists who specialize in "narrative therapy" focus their counseling approach on identifying harmful parts of a client's life story, and on helping them re-author newer and healthier stories.

Many of life's important activities are understood in terms of narrative. Political activity, for example, often involves seeing oneself as a character in the ongoing story of history, whether that story involves the defense and spreading of democracy, a Marxist vision of the workers' revolution, or the mobilization of human action toward the salvation of the global ecosystem. As an approach to religious activity, narrative theology is also growing in popularity within Christian circles, with an emphasis on seeing oneself as an active participant in God's creative and redemptive story.

As we pass through the education system, most of us are also exposed to the "story of science," in which humanity's understanding of the world grows through the application of the scientific method to accumulate facts, resulting in a better world. Though this description of science has been strongly challenged on a number of levels, some have embraced this narrative and explicitly see themselves as active participants in the story of scientific progress.

When I teach my course on Learning and Behavior Modification, for example, I use a particular behavioral psychology textbook precisely because it is so useful in demonstrating this worldview to my students. The authors present as clear an endorsement of the "story of science" as I have ever seen, with scientific progress (and the authors explicitly link scientific progress with society's overall progress) described as a straight line, with the dark, ignorant, and savage past at one end, and the enlightened utopian future at the other. They see themselves as using the science of behavioral psychology to contribute to humanity's movement from darkness into light, and they invite the reader to join them on their quest.

MacIntyre claims that "I can only answer the question 'What am I to do?' if I can answer the prior question 'Of what story or stories do I find myself a part?'" If that is the case, of what story or stories do you find yourself a part? What is your quest? This is where I can provide you with no clear answers.

One group of researchers found that, in general, adults who lived lives of service and concern for the next generation tend to organize their life stories around a five-part "commitment story." In this story, the adults reflected on blessings in their childhoods, spoke of early life experiences that caused them to become aware of the sufferings of others, steadfastly held to a personal moral code, showed a tendency to transform obstacles and unfortunate events into positive outcomes, and dedicated themselves to benefiting others.

Within that sequence, though, there exists the possibility for a great diversity of personal experiences. Childhood blessings, for example, could include a loving family, inborn talent, or helpful friends. Possible methods for working to improve the lives of others, contributing to the next generation, or benefiting society in general are innumerable. A martial artist may be a teacher, a fighter, a performer, a sage, a saint, an athlete, a soldier, or any number of possible venues for serving others. So the question of your own story requires an answer that you construct as you live it.

As we write our story, we play many roles. Those roles will interact with each other, and will influence the goals that we pursue and the way in which we pursue them. One thing is certain: if you have chosen the martial arts as a way of life, then you have cast yourself in the role of protector. This role is to be a significant part of your identity. It should influence the way that you see yourself. It should influence the way that you see others. In short, it should influence who you are.

It is for this reason that, although the virtues examined in this book (courage, justice, temperance, wisdom, and benevolence) are virtues that appear in most philosophical and theological literatures on the virtues, for us they remain uniquely warrior virtues. The courage of a Christian is not precisely the same as the courage of a Confucian, and a soldier's wisdom is not precisely the same as a schoolteacher's wisdom. Different roles in different life stories will cause the virtues to show themselves in different ways. The "spin" that warriors place on classic virtues is what makes them warrior virtues. It is in the way that we incorporate these traits into ourselves, the way in which we cultivate them, and the way that we put them to use, that they find their place in our stories.

Comte-Sponville makes the claim that perhaps the only real point of a book about the virtues is so that we can have some sort of description of the ideal, so that we can gauge an approximate distance between that ideal and our current condition. Do not be frustrated if you complete this book with the impression that you are woefully lacking in the virtues. I came to the same conclusion while writing it, examining the ideas of great thinkers both historical and current, and gauging my own actions against the standards presented. But examining the philosophical ideal at least provides a direction, and the contributions of positive psychology have the potential to lead to more systematic methods for self-cultivation in that desired direction. Comte-Sponville also reminds us that "thinking about the virtues will not make us virtuous," so we should all strive to keep the warrior virtues in mind as we live out the daily chapters in our stories. Like a physical strength, virtues grow through practice. So go practice. *Vincite virtute vera.*

> *Waste no more time arguing about*
> *what a good man should be. Be one.*
>
> Marcus Aurelius

References

Acton, H. B. (1970). *Kant's moral philosophy*. New York: Macmillan & Co.

Andreini, C. (1991). *Arete* to *virtus*: Virgil's redefinition of the epic hero. In A. W. H. Adkins, J. K. Lowrence, & C. K. Ihara (Eds.) *Human virtue and human excellence* (pp. 73-94). New York: Peter Lang Publishing, Inc.

Anglo, S. (2000). *The martial arts of renaissance Europe*. New Haven, CT: Yale University Press.

Arman, M., & Rehnsfeldt, A. (2006). The presence of love in ethical caring. *Nursing Forum, 41,* 4-12.

Aronson, E. (1992). The return of the repressed: Dissonance theory makes a comeback. *Psychological Inquiry, 3,* 303-311.

Asvaghosha. (1967). *The awakening of faith* (Y. S. Hakeda, Trans.). New York: Columbia University Press.

Axinn, S. (1984). *A moral military*. Philadelphia, PA: Temple University Press.

Ayduk, O., Mendoza-Denton, R., Mischel, W., Downey, G., Peake, P. K., & Rodriguez, M. (2000). Regulating the interpersonal self: Strategic self-regulation for coping with rejection sensitivity. *Journal of Personality and Social Psychology, 79,* 776-792.

Baldwin, J. D., & Baldwin, J. I. (2001). *Behavior principles in everyday life (4th edition)*. Upper Saddle River, NJ: Prentice Hall.

Bandura, A. (1969). Social learning of moral judgments. *Journal of Personality and Social Psychology, 11,* 275-279.

Bandura, A. (1973). *Aggression: A social learning analysis*. Englewood Cliffs, NJ: Prentice-Hall.

Bandura, A., Grusec, J. E., & Menlove, M. L. (1967). Vicarious extinction of avoidance behavior. *Journal of Personality and Social Psychology, 5,* 16-23.

Barak, A. (1990). Counselor training in empathy by a game procedure. *Counselor Education and Supervision, 29,* 170-186.

Barber, M. (1994). *The new knighthood: A history of the order of the temple*. Cambridge, UK: Cambridge University Press.

Barnfield, A. M. C. (2003). Observational learning in the martial arts studio: Instructors as models of positive behaviors. *Journal of Asian Martial Arts*, 12, 8-17.

Barrett, E. B. (1916). *Strength of will.* New York: P. J. Kennedy & Sons.

Bartholomew, C. G., & Goheen, M. W. (2004). *The drama of scripture: Finding our place in the biblical story.* Grand Rapids, MI: Baker Academic.

Batson, C. D. (1990). How social an animal? The human capacity for caring. *American Psychologist, 45*, 336-346.

Batson, C. D. (1991). *The altruism question: Toward a social-psychological answer.* Hillsdale, NJ: Lawrence, Erlebaum Associates.

Batson, C. D., Klein, T. R., Highberger, L., & Shaw, L. L. (1995). Immorality from empathy-induced altruism: When compassion and justice conflict. *Journal of Personality and Social Psychology, 68*, 1042-1054.

Batson C. D., Lishner, D. A., Carpenter, A., Dulin, L., Harjusola-Webb, S., Stocks, E. L., Gale, S., Hassan, O., & Sampat, B. (2003). "…As you would have them do unto you": Does imagining yourself in the other's place stimulate moral action? *Personality and Social Psychology Bulletin, 29*, 1190-1201.

Batson, C. D., & Shaw, L. L. (1991). Evidence for altruism: Toward a pluralism of prosocial motives. *Psychological Inquiry, 2*, 107-122.

Baumeister, R. F., Bratslavski, E., Muraven, M., & Tice, D. M. (1998). Ego depletion: Is the active self a limited resource? *Journal of Personality and Social Psychology, 74*, 1252-1265.

Baumeister, R. F., Campbell, J. D., Krueger, J. I., & Vohs, K. D. (2003). Does high self-esteem cause better performance, interpersonal success, happiness, or healthier lifestyles? *Psychological Science in the Public Interest, 4*, 1-44.

Baumeister, R. F., Gailliot, M., DeWall, C. N., & Oaten, M. (2006). Self-regulation and personality: How interventions increase regulatory success, and how depletion moderates the effects of traits on behavior. *Journal of Personality, 74*, 1773-1802.

Baumeister, R. F., & Exline, J. J. (1999). Virtue, personality, and social relations: Self-control as the moral muscle. *Journal of Personality, 67*, 1165-1194.

Becker, E. (1973). *The denial of death.* New York: Free Press.

Benedict of Nursia. (1966). *The rule of Saint Benedict: Translated with an introduction by Cardinal Gasquet.* New York: Cooper Square Publishers. (Original work ca. 530)

Ben-Ze'ev, A. (1993). The virtue of modesty. *American Philosophical Quarterly*, 30, 235-246.

Berges, S. (2006). The hardboiled detective as moralist: Ethics in crime fiction. In T. Chappell (Ed.), *Values and virtues: Aristotelianism in contemporary ethics* (212-225), Oxford: Clarendon Press.

Bernard of Clairvaux. (1963). *The steps of humility* (G. B. Burch, Trans.). Notre Dame, IN: University of Notre Dame Press. (Original work c.1129-1135).

Bi, L., & D'Agostino, F. (2004). The doctrine of filial piety: A philosophical analysis of the concealment case. *Journal of Chinese Philosophy, 31*, 451-467.

Blanco, E. G. (Trans). (1971). *The rule of the Spanish military order of St James*. Lieden, Netherlands: E. J. Brill. Original work 1307.

Bodiford, W. M. (2006). Neo-Confucianism and the Japanese martial arts. InYo: *Journal of Alternative Perspectives on the Martial Arts and Sciences*. Retrieved June 26, 2006 from http://ejmas.com/jalt/jaltframe.htm.

Brendtro, L. K., Brokenleg, M., & Van Bockern, S. (2005). The circle of courage and positive psychology. *Reclaiming Children and Youth, 14,* 130-136.

Brighouse, H. (2006). Justifying patriotism. *Social Theory and Practice, 32,* 547-558.

Brown, K. W., & Ryan, R. M. (2003). The benefits of being present: Mindfulness and its role in psychological well-being. *Journal of Personality and Social Psychology, 84,* 822-848.

Bruner, J. (2002). *Making stories: Law, literature, life*. New York: Farrar, Straus and Giroux.

Burdick, D. (1997). People & events of taekwondo's formative years. *Journal of Asian Martial Arts, 6,* 30-49.

Burton, R. F. (1987). *The book of the sword*. New York: Dover Publications Inc. (Original work published 1884)

Burtt, E. A. (Ed.). (1955). *The teachings of the compassionate Buddha*. New York: Mentor Books.

Buss, S. (1999). Appearing respectful: The moral significance of manners. *Ethics, 109,* 795-826.

Cain, A. (2005). Books and becoming good: Demonstrating Aristotle's theory of moral development in the act of reading. *Journal of Moral Education, 34,* 171-183.

Cameron, K. S., Bright, D., & Caza, A. (2004). Exploring the relationships between organizational virtuousness and performance. *American Behavioral Scientist, 47,* 766-790.

Carse, A. L. (2005). The moral contours of empathy. *Ethical Theory and Moral Practice, 8,* 169-195.

Carver, S. C, & Schier, M. F. (1982). Control theory: A useful conceptual framework for personality-social, clinical, and health psychology. *Psychological Bulletin, 92,* 111-135.

Cassell, E. J. (2005). Compassion. In C. R. Snyder & S. J. Lopez (Eds.), *Handbook of positive psychology* (pp. 434-445). New York: Oxford University Press.

Cheng, C. (2006). Preface: What is wisdom? *Journal of Chinese Philosophy, 33,* 317-318.

Chittick, W. C. (1996). Ibn 'Arabī. In S. H. Nasr & O. Leaman (Eds.) *History of Islamic philosophy* (pp. 497-509). New York: Routledge.

Cleary, T. (Trans.). (2008). *Training the samurai mind: A bushido sourcebook*. Boston: Shambhala Publications.

Cohen, D., Nisbett, R. E., Bowdle, B. F., & Schwarz, N. (1996). Insult, aggression, and the Southern culture of honor: An "experimental ethnography." *Journal of Personality and Social Psychology, 70,* 945-960.

Cohn, M. A. (2004). Rescuing our heroes: Positive perspectives on upward comparisons in relationships, education, and work. In P. A. Linley & S. Joseph (Eds.) *Positive psychology in practice* (pp. 218-237). Hoboken, NJ: John Wiley & Sons.

Coke, J. S., Batson, C. D., & McDavis, K. (1978). Empathic mediation of helping: A two-stage model. *Journal of Personality and Social Psychology, 36,* 752-766.

Cole, D. (1999). Thomas Aquinas on virtuous warfare. *Journal of Religious Ethics, 27,* 57-80.

Collins, J. D. (1962). *The lure of wisdom.* Milwaukee, WI: Marquette University Press.

Colvin, C. R., & Block, J. (1994). Do positive illusions foster mental health? An examination of the Taylor and Brown formulation. *Psychological Bulletin, 116,* 3-20.

Colvin, C. R., Block, J., & Funder, D. C. (1995). Overly positive self-evaluations and personality: Negative implications for mental health. *Journal of Personality and Social Psychology, 68,* 1152-1162.

Comte-Sponville, A. (2001). *A small treatise on the great virtues* (C. Temerson, Trans.). New York: Henry Holt & Company.

Conze, E. (1951). *Buddhism: Its essence and development.* New York: Philosophical Library.

Cooper, E. K. (2005). Using observational learning methods for martial arts teaching & training. *Journal of Asian Martial Arts, 14,* 8-21.

Creel, H. G. (1970). *What is Taoism?* Chicago: The University of Chicago Press.

Cupit, G. (1996). *Justice as fittingness.* Oxford: Clarendon Press.

Cvet, D. M. (2005). The measure of a master swordsman. *Journal of Western Martial Art.* Retrieved June 26, 2006 from http://ejmas.com/jwma.

da Costa, D., Nelson, T. M., Rudes, J., & Guterman, J. T. (2007). A narrative approach to body dysmorphic disorder. *Journal of Mental Health Counseling, 29,* 67-80.

Dahlsgaard, K., Peterson, C., & Seligman, M. E. P. (2005). Shared virtue: The convergence of valued human strengths across culture and history. *Review of General Psychology, 9,* 203-213.

Daniels, K., & Thornton, E. W. (1990). Analysis of the relationship between hostility and training in the martial arts. *Journal of Sports Sciences, 8,* 95-101.

Danner, D. D., Snowdon, D. A., & Friesen, W. V. (2001). Positive emotions in early life and longevity: Findings from the nun study. *Journal of Personality and Social Psychology, 80,* 804-813.

Davis, F. D., & Yi, M. Y. (2004). Improving computer skill training: Behavior modeling, symbolic mental rehearsal, and the role of knowledge structures. *Journal of Applied Psychology, 89,* 509-523.

Dawes, R. M (1998). The social usefulness of self-esteem: A skeptical view. *Harvard Mental Health Letter, 16,* 4-5.

Della Casa, G. (1958). *Galateo: Or the book of manners* (R. S. Pine-Coffin, trans.). Baltimore, MD: Penguin Press. (Original work published 1558)

Denney, D. R., & Sullivan, B. J. (1976). Desensitization and modeling treatments of spider fear using two types of scenes. *Journal of Consulting and Clinical Psychology, 44,* 573-579.

Diener, E. (1984). Subjective well-being. *Psychological Bulletin, 95,* 542-575.

Dijkerman, H. C., Letswaart, M., Johnston, M., & MacWalter, R.S. (2004). Does motor imagery training improve hand function in chronic stroke patients? A pilot study. *Clinical Rehabilitation, 18,* 538-549.

Dobson, T. (1985). A kind word turneth away wrath. In R. S. Heckler (Ed.), *Aikido and the new warrior* (pp. 65-69). Berkeley, CA: North Atlantic Books.

Dollard, J. (1944). *Fear in battle.* Washington, DC: Infantry Journal, Inc.

Donahue, J. J. (1994). *Warrior dreams: The martial arts and the American imagination.* Westport, CN: Bergin & Garvey.

Donahue, J. J. (2002). Wave people: The martial arts and the American imagination. In D. E. Jones (Ed.) *Combat, ritual, and performance: Anthropology of the martial arts* (pp. 65-80). Westport, CN: Praeger Publishers.

Driver, J. (1999). Modesty and ignorance. *Ethics, 109,* 827-834.

Dumas, A. (1931). *The three musketeers - with an introduction by Sidney Dark.* London: Collins'.

Eichler, L. (1923). *Book of etiquette.* Garden City, NY: Nelson Doubleday, Inc.

Eisenberg, N., Miller, P. A. (1987). The relation of empathy to prosocial and related behaviors. *Psychological Bulletin, 101,* 91-119.

Eisenberger, R. (1992). Learned industriousness. *Psychological Review, 99,* 248-267.

Fagin-Jones, S., & Midlarsky, E. (2007). Courageous altruism: Personal and situational correlates of rescue during the Holocaust. *The Journal of Positive Psychology, 2,* 136-147.

Fengyan, W. (2004). Confucian thinking in traditional moral education: Key ideas and fundamental features. *Journal of Moral Education, 33,* 429-447.

Feyerabend, P. (1993). *Against method (3rd edition).* New York: Verso.

Finkenberg, M. F. (1990). Effect of participation in taekwondo on college women's self-concept. *Perceptual and Motor Skills,71,* 891-894.

Fives, A. (2005). Virtue, justice, and the human good: Non-relative communitarian ethics and the life of religious commitment. *Contemporary Politics, 11,* 117-131.

Focht, B. C., Bouchard, L. J., Murphey, M. (2000). Influence of martial arts training on the perception of experimentally induced pressure pain and selected psychological responses. *Journal of Sport Behavior, 23,* 232-244.

Foot, P. (1978). *Virtues and vices and other essays in moral philosophy.* Berkley, CA: University of California Press.

Foot, P. (2001). *Natural goodness.* Oxford: Clarendon Press.

Fosdick, H. E. (1927). *The meaning of service.* New York: Association Press.

Fowers, B. J. (1998). Psychology and the good marriage: Social theory as practice. *American Behavioral Scientist, 41,* 516-541.

Fowers, B. J. (2005). *Virtue and psychology: Pursuing excellence in everyday practices.* Washington, DC: American Psychological Association.

Frankl, V. E. (1984). *Man's search for meaning: An introduction to logotherapy (3rd Edition).* New York: Simon & Schuster.

Frketich, J. (2006, November 21). No pandemic care for the elderly. *The Hamilton Spectator,* p. A1.

Funakoshi, G., & Nakasone, G. (2003). *The twenty guiding principles of karate: The spiritual legacy of the master* (J. Teramoto, trans.). Tokyo: Kodansha International. (Original work published 1938)

Gable, S. L., & Haidt, J. (2005). What (and why) is positive psychology? *Review of General Psychology, 9,* 103-10.

Gailliot, M. T., Schmeichel, B. J., & Baumeister, R. F. (2006). Self-regulatory processesdefend against the threat of death: Effects of self-control depletion and trait self-control on thoughts and fears of dying. *Journal of Personality and Social Psychology, 91,* 49-62.

Gard, R. A. (1962). *Buddhism.* New York: George Braziller Inc.

Gerber, L. (2002). Standing humbly before nature. *Ethics & the Environment, 7,* 39-53.

Gilligan, C. (1982). *In a different voice: Psychological theory and women's development.* Cambridge, MA: Harvard University Press.

Gleser, J., & Brown, P. (1988). Judo principles and practices: Applications to conflict-solving strategies in psychotherapy. *American Journal of Psychotherapy, 17,* 437-447.

Gleser, J. M., Margulies, J. Y., Nyeska, M., Porat, S., Mandelberg, H., & Wertman, E. (1992). Physical and psychosocial benefits of modified judo practice for blind, mentally retarded children: A pilot study. *Perceptual and Motor Skills, 74,* 915-925.

Goldberg, C., & Simon, J. (1982). Toward a psychology of courage: Implications for the change (healing) process. *Journal of Contemporary Psychotherapy, 13,* 107-128.

Gollwitzer, P. M. (1999). Implementation intentions: Strong effects of simple plans. *American Psychologist, 54,* 493-503.

Goud, N. H. (2005). Courage: Its nature and development. *Journal of Humanistic Counseling, Education and Development, 44,* 102-116.

Grayson, W. J. (1853). The character of the gentleman. *Southern Quarterly Review, 7,* 53-80.

Graziano, A. M., DeGiovanni, I. S., & Garcia, K. A. (1979). Behavioral treatment of children's fears: A review. *Psychological Bulletin, 86,* 804-830.

Greenberg, J., Solomon, S., & Pyszczynski, T. (1997). Terror management theory of self-esteem and cultural worldviews: Empirical assessments and conceptual refinements. In M. P. Zanna (Ed.), *Advances in experimental social psychology* (Vol. 29, pp. 61-139). San Diego: Academic Press.

Greenberg, K. (1990). The nose, the lie, and the duel in the antebellum south. *The American Historical Review, 95,* 57-74.

Gregg, R. C., & Groh, D. E. (1981). *Early arianism – A view of salvation.* Philadelphia, PA: Fortress Press.

Grenz, S. J. (1994). *Theology for the community of God.* Grand Rapids, MI: William B. Eerdmans Publishing Company.

Gunderson, M. (2004). A Kantian view of suicide and end-of-life treatment. *Journal of Social Philosophy, 35,* 277-287.

Habito, R. L. F. (2002). Compassion out of wisdom: Buddhist perspectives from the past toward the human future. In S. G. Post, L. G. Underwood, J. P. Schloss, & W. B. Hurlbut (Eds.), *Altruism and altruistic love: Science, philosophy, & religion in dialogue* (pp. 362-375). New York: Oxford University Press.

Hackney, C. H. (2006). Reflections on *audatia* as a martial virtue. *Journal of Western Martial Art.* Retrieved September 17th, 2006 from http://ejmas. com/jwma.

Hadaway, B. S. (2006). Preparing the way for justice: Strategic dispositional formation through the spiritual disciplines. *Journal of Education & Christian Belief, 10,* 143-165.

Harper, K. M. (2001). The environment as master narrative: Discourse and identity in environmental problems. *Anthropological Quarterly, 74,* 101-103.

Hatsumi, M. (1981). *Ninjutsu: History and tradition.* Burbank, CA: Unique Publications, Inc.

Hatsumi, M. (1988a). *Essence of ninjutsu: The nine traditions.* Chicago, IL: Contemporary Books.

Hatsumi, M. (1988b). *The grandmaster's book of ninja training.* Chicago, IL: Contemporary Books.

Hatsumi, M. (1998). *Ninpo: Wisdom for life* (H. Tokumitsu, N. Yokota, & J. Maurantonio, Trans). Yonkers, NY: Mushashin Press.

Hatsumi, M. (2005). *Japanese sword fighting: Secrets of the samurai* (B. Appleby & D. Wilson, Trans.). New York: Kodansha International.

Hatsumi, M., & Cole, B. (2001). *Understand? Good. Play!* USA: Bushin Books.

Hatzichronoglou, L. (1991). Theognis and *arete.* In A. W. H. Adkins, J. K. Lowrence, & C. K. Ihara (Eds.) *Human virtue and human excellence* (pp. 17-44). New York: Peter Lang Publishing, Inc.

Headley, B., & Wearing, A. (1987). The sense of relative superiority—central to well-being. *Social Indicators Research, 20,* 497-516.

Heinlein, R. A. (1959). *Starship troopers.* New York: G. P. Putman's Sons.

Held, V. (2006). *The ethics of care: Personal, political, and global.* New York: Oxford University Press.

Higgins, C. (2003). MacIntyre's moral theory and the possibility of an aretaic ethics of teaching. *Journal of Philosophy of Education, 37,* 279-292.

Hoban, J. E. (2007, Sept.). The ethical marine warrior: Achieving a higher standard. *Marine Corps Gazette,* 36-40.

Hoff, F. (2002). *Kyudo: The way of the bow* (S. C. Kohn, trans). Boston: Shambhala Publications Inc.

Hoorens, V. (1995). Self-favoring biases, self-presentation and the self-other asymmetry in social comparison. *Journal of Personality, 63,* 793-819.

Huang, Y. (2006). A neo-Confucian conception of wisdom: Wang Mingyang on the innate moral knowledge (*liangzhi*). *Journal of Chinese Philosophy, 33,* 393-408.

Hurst III, G. C. (1990). Death, honor, and loyalty: The bushido ideal. *Philosophy East and West, 40,* 511-528.

Hursthouse, R. (1999). *On virtue ethics.* Oxford: Oxford University Press.

Jones, H. E. (1971). *Kant's principle of personality.* Madison, WI: University of Wisconsin Press.

Jordan, R. D. (1989). *The quiet hero: Figures of temperance in Spenser, Donne, Milton, and Joyce.* Washington, DC: The Catholic University of America Press.

Kant, I. (1997). *Groundwork of the metaphysics of morals (M. Gregor, Trans.).* Cambridge, UK: Cambridge University Press.

Kateb, G. (2004). Courage as a virtue. *Social Research, 71,* 39-72.

Kauz, H. (1977). *The martial spirit: An introduction to the origin, philosophy, and psychology of the martial arts.* Woodstock, NY: The Overlook Press.

Keen, M. (1984). *Chivalry.* New Haven, CN: Yale University Press.

Keown, D. (2001). *The nature of Buddhist ethics.* New York: Palgrave.

Kimura, K. (1991). The self in medieval Japanese Buddhism: Focusing on Dogen. *Philosophy East & West, 41,* 327-341.

Kinsella, N. (1960). *Unprofitable servants: Conferences on humility.* Westminster, MD: Newman Press.

Kiyota, M. (2002). *The shambhala guide to kendo.* Boston: Shambhala Publications Inc.

Kohlberg, L. (1981). *The philosophy of moral development: Moral stages and the idea of justice.* San Francisco, CA: Harper & Row.

Kosits, R. D. (2004). Of faculties, fallacies, and freedom: Dilemma and irony in the secularization of American psychology. *History of Psychology, 7,* 340-366.

Kotva Jr., J. J. (1996). *The Christian case for virtue ethics.* Washington, DC: Georgetown University Press.

Krause, S. (2002). *Liberalism with honor.* Cambridge, MA: Harvard University Press.

Kristeller, J. R., & Johnson, T. (2005). Cultivating loving kindness: A two-stage model of the effects of meditation of empathy, compassion, and altruism. *Zygon, 40,* 391-407.

Kristjánsson, K. (2006). Emulation and the use of role models in moral education. *Journal of Moral Education, 35,* 37-49.

Kuhn, T. S. (1996). *The structure of scientific revolutions* (3rd edition). Chicago: University of Chicago Press.

Kurian, M., Caterino, L. C., & Kulhavy, R. W. (1993). Personality characteristics and duration of ATA taekwondo training. *Perceptual and Motor Skills, 76,* 363-366.

Kurian, M., Verdi, M. P., Caterino, L. C., & Kulhavy, R. W. (1994). Rating scales on the children's personality questionnaire to training time and belt rank in ATA taekwondo. *Perceptual and Motor Skills, 79,* 904-906.

La Caze, M. (2005). Love: That Indispensable Supplement: Irigaray and Kant on love and respect. *Hypatia, 20,* 92-114.

Lakes, K. D., & Hoyt, W. T. (2004). Promoting self-regulation through school-based martial arts training. *Applied Developmental Psychology, 25,* 283-302.

Larson, R., Jarrett, R., Hansen, D., Pearce, N., Sullivan, P., Walker, K., Watkins, N., & Wood, D. (2004). Organized youth activities as contexts for positive development. In P. A. Linley & S. Joseph (Eds.), *Positive psychology in practice* (pp. 540-560). Hoboken, NJ: John Wiley & Sons.

Layton, C. (1988). The personality of black-belt and nonblack-belt traditional karateka. *Perceptual and Motor Skills, 67,* 218.

Layton, C. (1990). Anxiety in black-belt and nonblack-belt traditional karateka. *Perceptual and Motor Skills, 71,* 905-906.

Lee, B. (1975). *The tao of jeet kun do.* Santa Clarita, CA: Ohara Publications, Inc.

Leming, J. S. (2000). Tell me a story: An evaluation of a literature-based character education programme. *Journal of Moral Education, 29,* 413-427.

Lewis, C. S. (2002). On the reading of old books. In W. Hooper (Ed.) *God in the dock: Essays on theology and ethics* (pp. 200-207). Grand Rapids, MI: William B. Eerdmans Publishing Company. (Original work published 1944)

Li, C. (1994). The Confucian concept of jen and the feminist ethics of care: A comparative study. *Hypatia, 9,* 70-89.

Liu, J. J. Y. (1961). The knight errant in Chinese literature. *Journal of the Hong Kong Branch of the Royal Asiatic Society, 1,* 30-41.

Liu, J. J. Y. (1967). *The Chinese knight-errant.* Chicago: The University of Chicago Press.

Livnat, Y. (2004). On the nature of benevolence. *Journal of Social Philosophy,35,* 304-317.

Loi, R., Hang-yue, N., & Foley, S. (2006). Linking employees' justice perceptions to organizational commitment and intention to leave: The mediating role of perceived organizational support. *Journal of Occupational and Organizational Psychology, 79,* 101-120.

Lovett, R., Davidson, M., & Lancaster, M. (Trans.). (2005). *Fiore dei Liberi project: Pisani-Dossi representation.* Retrieved July 6, 2006 from http://www.the-exiles.org/FioreProject/Project.htm.

Lowry, D. (1985). *Autumn lightning: The education of an American samurai.* Boston: Shambhala Publications.

Lowry, D. (1995). *Sword and brush: The spirit of the martial arts.* Boston: Shambhala Publications.

Lowry, D. (2000). *Moving toward stillness: Lessons in daily life from the martial ways of Japan.* Boston: Tuttle Publishing.

Lowry, D. (2006). *In the dojo: A guide to the rituals and etiquette of the Japanese martial arts.* Boston: Weatherhill.

Lubonja, F. (2004). Courage and the terror of death (J. Hodgson, trans.). *Social Research, 71,* 117-134.

Maas, A., Ceccarelli, R., & Rudin, S. (1996). Linguistic intergroup bias: Evidence for in-group-protective motivation. *Journal of Personality and Social Psychology, 71,* 512-526.

Machiavelli, N. (1947). *The prince* (T. G. Bergin, Trans.). New York: Appleton-Century-Crofts. (Original work published 1513).

MacIntyre, A. (1984). *After virtue (2nd Edition).* Notre Dame, IN: University of Notre Dame Press.

MacIntyre, A. (1988). *Whose justice? Which rationality?* Notre Dame, IN: University of Notre Dame Press.

MacIntyre, A. (1990). *Three rival versions of moral enquiry: Encyclopaedia, genealogy, and tradition.* Notre Dame, IN: University of Notre Dame Press.

Madden, M. E. (1990). Attributions of control and vulnerability at the beginning and end of a karate course. *Perceptual and Motor Skills, 70,* 787-794.

Madden, M. E. (1995). Perceived vulnerability and control of martial arts and physical fitness students. *Perceptual and Motor Skills, 80,* 899-910.

Maliszewski, M. (1996). *Spiritual dimensions of the martial arts.* Rutland, VT: Charles E. Tuttle Company.

Mandeville, B. (1732). *An enquiry into the origin of honour, and the usefulness of Christianity in war.* London: John Brotherton.

Mason, J. E. (1935). *Gentlefolk in the making: Studies in the history of English courtesy literature and related topics from 1531-1774.* Philadelphia, PA: University of Pennsylvania Press.

McAdams, D. P. (1999). Personal narratives and the life story. In L. A. Pervin & O. P. John (Eds), *Handbook of personality: Theory and research* (pp. 478-500). New York: The Guilford Press.

McAdams, D. P. (2001). The psychology of life stories. *Review of General Psychology, 5,* 100-122.

McAdams, D. P., Diamond, A., de St. Aubin, E., & Mansfield, E. (1997). Stories of commitment: The psychosocial construction of generative lives. *Journal of Personality and Social Psychology, 72,* 678-694.

McCullough, M. E., Bellah, C. G., Kilpatrick, S. D., Johnson, J. L. (2001). Vengefulness: Relationships with forgiveness, rumination, well-being, and the big five. *Personality and Social Psychology Bulletin, 27,* 601-610.

McCullough, M. E., & Witvliet, C. V. (2005). The psychology of forgiveness. In C. R. Snyder & S. J. Lopez (Eds.), *Handbook of positive psychology* (pp. 446-458). New York: Oxford University Press.

McKenna, F. P., & Myers, L. B. (1997). Illusory self-assessments—Can they be reduced? *British Journal of Psychology, 88,* 39-51.

McLaren, B. D. (2003). *The story we find ourselves in: Further adventures of a new kind of Christian.* San Francisco, CA: Jossey-Bass.

Menache, S. (1993). The templar order: A failed ideal? *Catholic Historical Review, 79,* 1-21.

Mezulis, A. H., Abramson, L. Y., Hyde, J. S., & Hankin, B. L. (2004). Is there a universal positivity bias in attributions? A meta-analytic review of individual, developmental, and cultural differences in the self-serving attributional bias. *Psychological Bulletin, 130,* 711-747.

Milgram, S. (1974). *Obedience to authority.* New York: Harper & Row.

Miller, J. (2003). *Daoism: A short introduction.* Oxford: Oneworld Publications.

Miller, P. A., & Eisenberg, N. (1988). The relation of empathy to aggressive and externalizing/antisocial behavior. *Psychological Bulletin, 103,* 324-344.

Miller, R. S., & Schlenker, B. R. (1985). Egotism in group members: Public and private attributions of responsibility for group performance. *Social Psychology Quarterly, 48,* 85-89.

Miller, W. R., & DiPilato, M. (1983). Treatment of nightmares via relaxation and desensitization: A controlled evaluation. *Journal of Consulting and Clinical Psychology, 51,* 870-877.

Mischel, W., & Baker, N. (1975). Cognitive appraisals and transformations in delay behavior. *Journal of Personality and Social Psychology, 31,* 254-261.

Mischel, W., & Ebbesen, E. B. (1970). Attention in delay of gratification. *Journal of Personality and Social Psychology, 16,* 329-337.

Mischel, W., Ebbesen, E. B., & Zeiss, A. R. (1972). Cognitive and attentional mechanisms in delay of gratification. *Journal of Personality and Social Psychology, 21,* 204-218.

Monroe, K. R. (1996). *The heart of altruism: Perceptions of a common humanity.* Princeton, NJ: Princeton University Press.

Morgan, B., Morgan, F., Foster, V., & Kolbert, J. (2000). Promoting the moral and conceptual development of law enforcement trainees: A deliberate psychological education approach. *Journal of Moral Education, 29,* 203-218.

Morgan, F. E. (1992). *Living the martial way.* New York: Barricade Books.

Munenori, Y. (2005). Martial arts: The book of family traditions. In T. Cleary (Ed., Trans.) *Soul of the samurai* (pp. 8-99). North Clarendon, VT: Tuttle Publishing.

Muraven, M., & Baumeister, R. F. (2000). Self-regulation and depletion of limited resources: Does self-control resemble a muscle? *Psychological Bulletin, 126,* 247-259.

Muraven, M., Baumeister, R. F., & Tice, D. M. (1999). Longitudinal improvement of self-regulation through practice: Building self-control strength through repeated exercise. *The Journal of Social Psychology, 139,* 446-457.

Muraven, M., Tice, D. M., & Baumeister, R. F. (1998). Self-control as limited resource: Regulatory depletion patterns. *Journal of Personality and Social Psychology, 74,* 774-789.

Murdoch, I. (1970). *The sovereignty of good.* London: Routledge & Kegan Paul.

Murphy, N. (2005). Theological resources for integration. In A. Dueck & C. Lee (Eds), *Why psychology needs theology: A radical-reformation perspective* (pp 28-52). Grand Rapids, MI: William B. Eerdmans Publishing Company.

Murphy, N., & Ellis, G. F. R. (1996). *On the moral nature of the universe: Theology, cosmology, and ethics.* Minneapolis, MN: Fortress Press.

Murray, A. (1920). *Humility: The beauty of holiness.* New York: Fleming H. Revell Company.

Musashi, M. (1994). *The martial artist's book of five rings* (S. F. Kaufman, Trans.). Boston: Charles E. Tuttle Co. (Original work published 1645)

Nelson, R. F. (Ed.). (1989). *The overlook martial arts reader: An anthology of historical and philosophical writings.* Woodstock, NY: The Overlook Press.

Nettleship, R. L. (1961). *Lectures on the republic of Plato (2nd edition).* New York: St Martin's Press. (Original work published 1901).

Nitobe, I. (1969). *Bushido: The soul of Japan.* Rutland, VT: Charles E. Tuttle Company. (Original work published 1905).

North, H. F. (1979). *From myth to Icon: Reflections of Greek ethical doctrine in literature and art.* Ithaca, NY: Cornell University Press.

Nosanchuk, T. A. (1981). The way of the warrior: The effects of traditional martial arts training on aggressiveness. *Human Relations, 34,* 435-444.

Nuyen, A. T. (2004). The contemporary relevance of the Confucian idea of filial piety. *Journal of Chinese Philosophy, 31,* 433-450.

Oaten, M., & Cheng, K. (2006). Longitudinal gains in self-regulation from regular physical exercise. *British Journal of Health Psychology, 11,* 717-733.

Oh, D. (2007, January). *The relevance of virtue ethics and application to the formation of character development in warriors.* Paper presented at the International Symposium for Military Ethics, Springfield, IV.

Okazaki, T. (2006). *Perfection of character: Guiding principles for the martial arts & everyday life.* Philadelphia, PA: GMW Publishing.

Olson, R. (2006). *Arminian theology: Myths and realities.* Downers Grove, IL: InterVarsity Press.

Olsthoorn, P. (2005). Honor as a motive for making sacrifices. *Journal of Military Ethics, 4,* 183-197.

Opotow, S., Gerson, J., & Woodside, S. (2005). From moral exclusion to moral inclusion: Theory for teaching justice. *Theory Into Practice, 44,* 303-318.

Order of Shaolin Ch'an. (2004). *The Shaolin grandmasters' text: History, philosophy, and gung fu of Shaolin Ch'an.* Beaverton, OR: Tuttle Publishing.

Parish, T. S., Buntman, A. D., & Buntman, S. R. (1976). Effects of counterconditioning on test anxiety as indicated by digit span performance. *Journal of Educational Psychology, 68,* 297-299.

Paulhus, D. (1998). Interpersonal and intrapsychic adaptiveness of trait self-enhancement: A mixed blessing? *Journal of Personality and Social Psychology, 74,* 1197-1208.

Peterson, C. (2006). *Follow-up Q & A with Chris Peterson* (audio recording). Retrieved June 27, 2006 from http://www.coachingtowardhappiness.com/archive/peterson.htm.

Peterson, C., & Seligman, M. E. P. (2004). *Character strengths and virtues: A handbook and classification.* Washington, DC: American Psychological Association.

Pieper, J. (1965). *The four cardinal virtues.* New York: Harcourt, Brace & World, Inc.

Post, E. (1927). *Etiquette (new and enlarged edition).* New York: Funk & Wagnalls Company.

Post, S. G. (2002). The tradition of agape. In S. G. Post, L. G. Underwood, J. P. Schloss, & W. B. Hurlbut (Eds.), *Altruism and altruistic love: Science, philosophy, & religion in dialogue* (pp. 51-64). New York: Oxford University Press.

Pyszczynski, T., Solomon, S., & Greenberg, J. (2002). *In the wake of 9/11: The psychology of terror.* Washington, DC: American Psychological Association.

Raterman, T. (2006). On modesty: Being good and knowing it without flaunting it. *American Philosophical Quarterly, 43,* 221-232.

Ratti, O., & Westbrook, A. (1973). *Secrets of the samurai: A survey of the martial arts of feudal Japan.* Rutland, VT: Charles E Tuttle Company.

Rawls, J. (1971). *A theory of justice.* Cambridge, MA: Harvard University Press.

Reznitskaya, A., & Sternberg, R. J. (2004). Teaching students to make wise judgments: The "teaching for wisdom" program. In P. A. Linley & S. Joseph (Eds.), *Positive psychology in practice* (pp. 181-196). Hoboken, NJ: John Wiley & Sons, Inc.

Rice, E. (1958). *The renaissance idea of wisdom.* Cambridge, MA: Harvard University Press.

Richards, N. (1988). Is humility a virtue? *American Philosophical Quarterly, 25,* 253-259.

Richman, C. L., & Rehberg, H. (1986). The development of self-esteem through the martial arts. *International Journal of Sport Psychology, 17,* 234-239.

Riegel, K. (2005). Marxism-Leninism as a political religion. *Totalitarian Movements and Political Religions, 6,* 97-126.

Robazza, C., Bortoli, L., & Nougier, V. (1998). Physiological arousal and performance in elite archers: A field study. *European Psychologist, 3,* 263-270.

Roberts, R. C. (1995). Forgivingness. *American Philosophical Quarterly, 32,* 289-306.

Rodriguez, M. L., Mischel, W., & Shoda, Y. (1989). Cognitive person variables in the delay of gratification of older children at risk. *Journal of Personality and Social Psychology, 57,* 358-367.

Royce, J. (1924). *The philosophy of loyalty.* New York: The Macmillan Company.

Ruiz, P. R., & Vallejos, R. M. (1999). The role of compassion in moral education. *Journal of Moral Education, 28,* 5-17.

Ruth, J. A. (1880). *Decorum: A practical treatise on etiquette and dress of the best American society*. New York: Union Publishing House.

Sadeghi, A. (2004). Hero and heroism in the *Shahnameh* and the *Masnavi*. *Critique: Critical Middle Eastern Studies, 13*, 195-208.

Saposnek, D. T. (1985). Aikido: A model for brief strategic therapy. In R. S. Heckler (Ed.) *Aikido and the new warrior* (pp. 178-197). Berkeley, CA: North Atlantic Books.

Schaff, P. (1995). *History of the Christian church, Volume II: Ante-nicene Christianity (3rd edition)*. Grand Rapids, MI: William B. Eerdmans Publishing Company. (Original work published 1910)

Schueler, G. F. (1997). Why modesty is a virtue. *Ethics, 107*, 467-485.

Schuler, R. (1969). *Self-love: The dynamic force of success*. New York: Hawthorne Books, Inc.

Schuler, R. (1982). *Self-esteem: The new reformation*. Waco, TX: Key-Word Books.

Seligman, M. E. P. (1999). The president's address. *American Psychologist, 54*, 559-562.

Seligman, M. E. P. (2002). *Authentic happiness: Using the new positive psychology to realize your potential for lasting fulfillment*. New York: Free Press.

Seligman, M. E. P., & Csikszentmihalyi, M. (2000). Positive psychology: An introduction. *American Psychologist, 55*, 5-14.

Seward, D. (1972). *The monks of war: The military religious orders*. London: Eyre Methuen Ltd.

Shapiro, J., Morrison, E. H., & Boker, J. R. (2004). Teaching empathy to first year medical students: Evaluation of an elective literature and medicine course. *Education for Health, 17*, 73-84.

Shapiro, J., & Rucker, L. (2004). The Don Quixote effect: Why going to the movies can help develop empathy and altruism in medical students and residents. *Families, Systems, & Health, 22*, 445-452.

Sidney, A. (1989). *A moral military*. Philadelphia, PA: Temple University Press.

Silver, G. (1599). *Paradoxes of defense*. Retrieved November 10, 2004 from http://www.aemma.org/onlineResources/silver.

Silver, G. (1605). *Brief instructions to my paradoxes of defense*. Retrieved November 10, 2004 from http://www.aemma.org/onlineResources/silver.

Singer, S. J. (2005). Educating for commitment: Insights from postmodernity. *Religious Education, 100*, 296-310.

Sivanathan, N., Arnold, K. A., Turner, N., & Barling, J. (2004). Leading well: Transformational leadership and well-being. In A. Linley & S, Joseph (Eds), *Positive Psychology in Practice*, 241-255. Hoboken, NJ: Wiley.

Skelton, D. L., Glynn, M. A., & Berta, S. M. (1991). Aggressive behavior as a function of taekwondo ranking. *Perceptual and Motor Skills, 72*, 179-182.

Slater, J., & Hunt, H. T. (1997). Postural-vestibular integration and forms of dreaming: A preliminary report on the effects of brief t'ai chi chuan training. *Perceptual and Motor Skills, 85*, 97-98.

Slingerland, E. (2001). Virtue ethics, the *Analects*, and the problem of commensurability. *Journal of Religious Ethics, 29,* 97-125.

Smith, R. (2004, June). *The mission to promote liberty around the world: American civic identity and universal rights.* Paper presented at the annual meeting of the American Political Science Association. Chicago, IL.

Soho, T. (2005). The inscrutable subtlety of immovable wisdom. T. Cleary (Ed.), *Soul of the samurai,* 100-141. North Clarendon, VT: Tuttle Publishing.

Sorokin, P. A. (1950). Love: Its aspects, production, transformation, and accumulation. In P. A. Sorokin (Ed.), *Explorations in altruistic love and behavior* (pp. 3-73). Boston: The Beacon Press.

Soyeshima, Y. (1927). *The essence of bushido.* Tokyo: The Herald Press.

Speicher, B. (1994). Family patterns of moral judgment during adolescence and young adulthood. *Developmental Psychology, 30,* 624-632.

Sprecher, S., & Fehr, B. (2005). Compassionate love for close others and humanity. *Journal of Social and Personal Relationships, 22,* 629-651.

Stack, C. B. (1993). The culture of gender: Women and men of color. In M. J. Larrabee (Ed.), *An ethic of care: Feminist and interdisciplinary perspectives* (pp. 108-111). New York: Routledge.

Staudinger, U. M., & Baltes, P. B. (1996). Interactive minds: A facilitative setting for wisdom-related performance? *Journal of Personality and Social Psychology, 71,* 746-762.

Sterba, J. P. (1988). *How to make people just: A practical reconciliation of alternate conceptions of justice.* Totowa, NJ: Rowman & Littlefield.

Sternberg, R. J. (Ed.). (1990). *Wisdom: Its nature, origins, and development.* New York: Cambridge University Press.

Sternberg, R. J. (1998). A balance theory of wisdom. *Review of General Psychology, 2,* 347-365.

Sternberg, R. J. (2001). Why schools should teach for wisdom: The balance theory of wisdom in educational settings. *Educational Psychologist, 36,* 227-245.

Sternberg, R. J. (2004). Why smart people can be so foolish. *European Psychologist, 9,* 145-150.

Stohr, K. (2006). Manners, morals, and practical wisdom. In T. Chappell (Ed.), *Values and virtues: Aristotelianism in contemporary ethics* (pp. 189-211). Oxford: Clarendon Press.

Strack, F., Martin, L. L., & Stepper, S. (1988). Inhibiting and facilitating conditions of the human smile: A nonobtrusive test of the facial feedback hypothesis. *Journal of Personality and Social Psychology, 54,* 768-777.

Sun Tzu. (1996). *The art of war.* (Stephen F Kaufman, Trans.) Rutland, VT: Charles E. Tuttle.

Sundararajan, L. (2005, August). *Beyond hope: The Chinese Buddhist notion of emptiness.* Paper presented at the annual convention of the American Psychological Association, Washington, DC.

Swearer, D. K. (1998). Buddhist virtue, voluntary poverty, and extensive benevolence. *Journal of Religious Ethics, 26,* 71-103.

Sweet, M. J., & Johnson, C. G. (1990). Enhancing empathy: the interpersonal implications of a Buddhist meditation technique. *Psychotherapy, 27,* 19-29.

Tangney, J. P. (2000). Humility: Theoretical perspectives, empirical findings and directions for future research. *Journal of Social and Clinical Psychology, 19,* 70-82.

Tangney, J. P., Baumeister, R. F., & Boone, A. L. (2004). High self-control predicts good adjustment, less pathology, better grades, and interpersonal success. *Journal of Personality, 72,* 271-324.

Targ, N. (2005). Fannie Lou Hamer (1917-1977). *Human Rights: Journal of the Section of Individual Rights and Responsibilities, 32,* C4.

Taylor, S. E., & Brown, J. D. (1988). Illusion and well-being: A social psychological perspective on mental health. *Psychological Bulletin, 103,* 193-210.

Telushkin, J. (2006). *A Jewish code of ethics: You shall be holy.* New York: Bell Tower.

Tikhonov, V. (1998). Hwarang organization: Its function and ethics. *Korea Journal, 38,* 318-338.

Toner, C. (2006). Military service as a practice: Integrating the sword and shield approaches to military ethics. *Journal of Military Ethics, 5,* 183-200.

Tronto, J. C. (1993). Beyond gender difference to a theory of care. In M. J. Larrabee (Ed.), *An ethic of care: Feminist and interdisciplinary perspectives* (240-257). New York: Routledge.

Trungpa, C. (1995). *Shambhala: The sacred path of the warrior.* Boston, MA: Shambhala Publications, Inc.

Trussell, R. P. (1978). Use of graduated behavior rehearsal, feedback, and systematic desensitization for speech anxiety. *Journal of Counseling Psychology, 25,* 14-20.

Tsunetomo, Y. (1983). *Hagakure: The book of the samurai.* (W. S. Wilson, Trans.). New York: Kodansha International. (Original work published 1716)

Twemlow, S. W., & Sacco, F. C. (1998). The application of traditional martial arts practice and theory to the treatment of violent adolescents. *Adolescence, 33,* 505-518.

Vale, M. (1981). *War and chivalry.* London: Gerald Duckworth & Co, Ltd.

von Leyden, W. (1985). *Aristotle on equality and justice: His political argument.* New York: St Martin's Press.

Vohs, K. D., & Baumeister, R. F. (2004). Understanding self-regulation: An introduction. In R. F. Baumeister & K. D. Vohs (Eds.)*Handbook of self-regulation: Research, theory, and applications* (pp. 1-12). New York: The Guilford Press.

Weary Bradley, G. (1978). Self-serving biases in the attribution process: A reexamination of the fact or fiction question. *Journal of Personality and Social Psychology, 36,* 56-71.

Weber, E. (1999). The ups and downs of honor. *American Scholar, 68,* 79-91.

Weiser, M., Kutz, I., Kutz, S. J., & Weiser, D. (1995). Psychotherapeutic aspects of the martial arts. *American Journal of Psychotherapy, 49,* 118-127.

Westhusing, T. (2003). A beguiling military virtue: honor. *Journal of Military Ethics, 2,* 195-212.

Wink, P., & Helson, R. (1997). Practical and transcendent wisdom: Their nature and some longitudinal findings. *Journal of Adult Development, 4,* 1-15.

Wyatt-Brown, B. (1982). *Southern honor: Ethics and behavior in the Old South.* New York: Oxford University Press.

Yearley, L. H. (1990). *Mencius and Aquinas: Theories of virtue and conceptions of courage.* Albany, NY: State University of New York Press.

Zivin, G., Hassan, N. R., DePaula, G. F., Monti, D. A., Harlan, C., Hossain, K. D., & Patterson, K. (2001). An effective approach to violence prevention: Traditional martial arts in middle school. *Adolescence, 36,* 443-459.

Index